John Ashbrook

The Pocket Essential

BRIAN DE PALMA

C000163379

www.pocketessentials.com

First published in Great Britain 2000 by Pocket Essentials, 18 Coleswood Road, Harpenden, Herts, AL5 1EQ

Distributed in the USA by Trafalgar Square Publishing, P.O. Box 257, Howe Hill Road, North Pomfret, Vermont 05053

Copyright © John Ashbrook 2000
Series Editor: Paul Duncan

A CIP catalogue record for this book is available from the British Library.

ISBN 1-903047-12-9

9 8 7 6 5 4 3 2 1

Book typeset by Lies
Printed and bound by Cox & Wyman

Dedicated to my first Film Studies teacher, Tim Farr, who showed me that watching films and then re-watching them, can be perfectly respectable way to pass the time. And to my parents, for the vast amounts of shelf space and infinite amounts of patience, I can merely say: "Hi mom!."

Big up an' nuff respeck to my homies:
Bill Fentum, whose wisdom and generosity proved extraordinarily helpful in the flurry to get this book finished (almost) on time. He and his website at 'briandepalma.net' provided me with vast quantities of information, far too much of which I deeply regret not having had the space to include.
Also, a begrudging, barely perceptible nod in the general direction of Richard Luck, who knows his rabbit at least as well as his monkey (sic).
Then there's Colin'n'Mitch'n'Sam'n'Anthony, who allowed me to raid some of the most obscure video collections on earth.
And, as ever, to Ellen and Steve for their piles... of research material.
Peace.

Contents

Brian De Palma: The Man Who Knew Too Much........................7

The Sixties: Be Black, Baby..16

Short Subjects, The Wedding Party, More Shorts, Murder À La Mod, Greetings, Hi Mom!

The Seventies: Burn In Hell..28

Dionysus In '69, Get To Know Your Rabbit, Sisters, Phantom Of The Paradise, Obsession, Carrie, The Fury, Home Movies

The Eighties: When You Get The Money, You Get The Power!...50

Dressed To Kill, Blow Out, Scarface, Body Double, Wise Guys, The Untouchables, Casualties Of War

The Nineties: Shake Hands With The Devil...............................71

The Bonfire Of The Vanities, Raising Cain, Carlito's Way, Mission:Impossible, Snake Eyes

The Noughties: Hello, Beautiful...................................86

Mission To Mars

Resource Materials...89

Filmography, Bibliography, Websites

Brian De Palma: The Man Who Knew Too Much

There is a signature to a Brian De Palma film which makes him as much of a conspicuous figure in his movies as his far-more publicity-hungry contemporaries Martin Scorsese and Steven Spielberg are in theirs. No matter which genre he works in, he leaves his fingerprints all over his films because he exerts so much control over every frame. He doesn't necessarily hold the cameras himself, and he certainly doesn't cut the film himself, but he surrounds himself with talented technicians with whom he has worked time and again, and who know his style almost as well as he does.

Over three decades of experimentation and consolidation, De Palma has discovered Robert De Niro and Jill Clayburgh when they were still teenagers. He gave Michelle Pfeiffer and Melanie Griffiths their career-altering roles. He boosted the fledgling careers of John Lithgow, F Murray Abraham, Kevin Costner, Andy Garcia and John Leguizamo . He gave John Travolta and Tom Hanks their first serious roles. He was instrumental in the rehabilitation of Sean Penn. He put Al Pacino and Sean Connery right back on the Hollywood A-list.

He also re-familiarised the world with the works of Alfred Hitchcock at a time when cinemas were dying-out and the video recorder had yet to make its way into many people's houses.

De Palma became an overnight success in 1996, with *Mission:Impossible*, after only 23 movies and 32 years. Finally he lost his 'rebellious' image, and was recognised as the skilled, fearsomely intelligent and, above all-else, technically proficient film-maker he truly is.

In the pre-title sequence of *Mission:Impossible*, we are introduced to star/icon Tom Cruise when he tears off a rubber mask, revealing the fresh-faced all-American we have come to know and expect. Brian De Palma has also torn away a mask, to reveal an inner person, simpler but arguably more attractive than before.

The old De Palma would not have been capable of steering a simplistic big-budget extravaganza like *Mission:Impossible* to the screen, he would have darkened and deepened it as a matter of course. But maintaining artistic integrity is obviously not enough. He lives in the land of opportunity and can't help but notice that it hasn't knocked as loud as on his friends' doors: "It's frustrating to have a success and not a blockbuster. I'm surrounded by associates who have monster hits"[1] Since his associates include Spielberg, Scorsese and George Lucas, you can see his point!

After his first bust-up with mainstream Hollywood, over the curio *Get To Know Your Rabbit*, De Palma realised something very important: Track record means nothing. He had made 5 independent movies, almost single-handedly. The doyenne of American film-criticism, Pauline Kael had praised his work (and continued to do so). But no one cared. In Hollywood he was no one because he had made them no money.

This was why he chose to move into genre pictures with the thriller *Sisters*. It would give him a chance to explore his interests in visual grammar – in telling stories with camera moves and editing rather than with dialogue – whilst giving Hollywood something that it could recognise and sell.

After 30-plus years, De Palma's love/hate relationship with Hollywood seems to have reached an uncomfortable accord. As Julie Salamon puts it in her excellent book *The Devil's Candy*: '(De Palma) was governed by conflicting impulses. He wanted to be recognised as an artist by the critical establishment, and he wanted to achieve box-office success. Yet his most personal films could never have the mass appeal of more conventional movies. When he followed his own instincts, he made movies that were almost guaranteed to offend.'[2]

Although he is traditionally seen as a Hollywood outsider, because he is forever ploughing his own furrow, this is, in point of fact, very far from the truth. Despite living and (whenever possible) working in New York, De Palma is a central figure in the off-screen life of Hollywood. His best friend in all the world is Steven Spielberg, and he is godfather to Spielberg's eldest son.

Spielberg is the very heart of Hollywood. No film gets made without him getting first refusal on the script. Any film he adds his producer credit to is guaranteed the widest-possible audience. Yet he admires De Palma's independence. When De Palma was making his first tentative steps back into the mainstream, with *Bonfire*, Spielberg understood the studio executives' fears: ".. a lot of these executives remember how Brian got his start, making Brian De Palma movies... that come from his soul, that come from who he is. Brian now has to take who he is and superimpose it on a movie that could have been made by Sidney Pollack, or Robert Benton, or Roman Polanski, John Schlesinger... each of these people would have made it different, but they all could have made *Bonfire Of The Vanities*. None of these people could have made *Obsession*. None of these people could have made *Dressed To Kill* or *Blow Out* or *Sisters*. None of them."[2]

Traditionally, Brian De Palma doesn't feel, he thinks. This is an attribute which has become increasingly uncommon in film-makers as post-modernism and the influence of Messrs Spielberg and Lucas take ever greater hold. Films no longer tell, they just show, they are proud to evoke emotion over cognition every time, yet this isn't and has never been enough for De Palma.

Whereas the Lucasfilm and Amblin (now DreamWorks) empires have been built on a bedrock of Saturday morning matinees and pulp fictions, De Palma (who has always resisted the temptation of creating a corporate vanity label under which to umbrella his films) always drew inspiration from 'higher' forms of film - initially the audacity of Welles and the new-wave verité of Jean-Luc Godard and Michelangelo Antonioni, then increasingly and more blatantly from the manipulative mastery of Hitchcock.

The practical upshot of this clinical precision was a series of films not so-much about people but about set-pieces. Separate high gloss pearls strung together by thin threads of plot. Certainly, the movies of his more successful contemporaries build to their spectacular highs - what are the shark attacks in *Jaws* or the T-Rex attack in *Jurassic Park* or the Death Star trench in *Star Wars* or the light-sabre duel in *Episode One*, if they aren't set-pieces to which the films have carefully steered us? The difference is that the techniques employed in family films are simpler and the tension more reliant on the audience's empathy for the characters. During his Hitchcock phase, this was not a consideration for De Palma.

Then things changed with *Scarface*. This was very much a film about people with frailties, and it led to a different kind of drama. Human drama. De Palma had seemingly finished 'learning' about what Hitchcock termed 'visual grammar,' and was now finding new ways to apply it.

Film is not a passive medium for De Palma. He doesn't want the audience to sit there, munching popcorn, brain idling, eyes wide; he wants active involvement and appreciation, and wishes more directors would refrain from taking the easy and populist way out: "Do you really want to go to work each day and shoot two-shots of people talking to each other?... That's not directing, it's being asleep at the switch. When you can put the camera anywhere and you can make it do anything, it's like you can put anything on that canvas. Well, why not think about it a bit?"[3]

This is why his early films are among the handful made in America to feature sparkling use of split-screen and multiple perspectives. The same murder filmed in 3 radically different styles in *Murder À La Mod*, a bomb

9

being planted behind stage, on one side of the screen, whilst the unsuspecting band continue to sing, on the other. Such techniques give the audience more information than the characters (which was one of the techniques identified by Hitchcock for generating suspense) as well as pushing the compliant viewers back into their seat and reminding them that they are watching a movie. After all, there's no point in being this good, if no one sits back for a moment and notices!

Never satisfied to merely grab an audience, De Palma will throw in distancing devices right at the height of the tension - such as the climactic burial sequence in *Body Double* when Craig Wasson, fighting for his life as the villain attempts to plant him 6 feet under, suddenly segues in his mind (but on our screen) to the pretend burial scene we saw on a movie set earlier. Here, Wasson decides to face up to his crippling claustrophobia and, with that decision, suddenly cuts back to the real confrontation. Another way of deliberately interrupting the suspension of disbelief is through the blatant allusion to another film. Why else does De Palma cut away from Margot Kidder's knife-murder in *Sisters* to watch the shadow of the knife stabbing the wall, as Bernard Herrmann reworks his *Psycho* strings? Why else does he interrupt the climactic shoot-out in *The Untouchables* with a slow motion retread of *Battleship Potemkin*'s Odessa Steps scene? He cannot take pride in getting the audience excited about the incident, they have to get excited about the technique, about the visual grammar.

"Audiences are very much used to being told what they are going to see and feel, so they're very comfortable with that... But when you make a film that plays with form it throws a lot of people off. They're not used to playing with form the way we did in the 60s and 70s with Godard or Antonioni."[3]

In interview, De Palma comes across as humourless and evasive. He obviously does not enjoy explaining himself, but is constantly required to do so because it is almost unprecedented in cinema for a credible and talented professional to have based so much of his work around that of another. Although he perpetually rejects claims that he has built his career on plagiarising Hitchcock, he cannot and indeed does not deny the obvious and deliberate debt he owes: "I wanted to make films based on visual grammar, and Hitchcock is the master of visual grammar, so I made a whole bunch of films based on Hitchcock story ideas, Hitchcock visual ideas, and basically learned the grammar."[4]

Of course, this alone doesn't explain why 'a whole bunch' should have kept him busy from *Sisters* in '71 through to *Raising Cain* over 20 years later but, as ever, he has a rehearsed answer ready for anyone who thinks to bring this up: "Hitchcock made 50 movies and explored every kind of visual grammar of suspense and action. So somewhere, if you're working with this type of visual storytelling, you're going to be using material Hitchcock has used before... It's almost impossible not to fall into his grammar, which is, of course, the best."[3]

Thanks largely to De Palma's influence, the point of view (POV) shot is a mainstay of cheap horror films, serving to focus the audience's attention on whatever atrocity the viewpoint character is committing, as well as disguising said character's identity. For De Palma it is, inevitably, far more than a stylistic conceit. By cutting the character out of the frame and simply allowing you to see what they see, you can temporarily inhabit their space "..instead of just using the camera as an objective recording device for dramatic action. Voyeurism is a direct link with a point of view shot."[1]

In common with his absent father, Hitchcock, De Palma is unrepentant about his fascination with the theme of voyeurism. It opens *Sisters* with the bizarre *You've Been Framed*-type game show, *Peeping Toms*. Then, half an hour later, the story suddenly hangs a left into horror territory with the journalist in the opposite building watching a murder victim clawing at a window with bloody fingers. This is clearly a reference to *Rear Window*, taken several steps further. He uses an identical set up in *Body Double* when Craig Wasson lasciviously uses a telescope initially to spy on his masturbating neighbour, then later to see an armed attacker waiting for her upstairs.

This interest in surveillance stretches back into De Palma's own troubled childhood. *The Devil's Candy* explores De Palma's turbulent family background in detail: 'The son of a depressed, overbearing mother and an aloof, physician father, De Palma spent his childhood in Philadelphia competing with his older brothers, Bruce – his parents' favourite – and Bart.'[2]

When Brian was in his teens, he learned that his father was being unfaithful, so set about following him and recording his activities, in an attempt to find him in flagrante delicto. This culminated in the 16-year-old Brian executing a commando-style raid on his father's offices one night. In this way, the 2 characters played by Keith Gordon, firstly in *Home Movies*, then in *Dressed To Kill*, most closely resemble De Palma himself. Indeed, *Home Movies* is a fictionalised account of this period in Brian's life.

De Palma sees the job of directing as epitomising both the voyeuristic side to his work, and the dualistic side: "Directing is standing behind the camera and watching what other people do... You have to make things happen and then you have to sit back and see what you have created in order to make it effective, you have to be detached. So it's a schizophrenic profession."[3]

Conflicting identities in a single body has been a perpetual theme of De Palma's work and, it seems, his working practice. It is a theme lifted from *Psycho*, but explored more fully in the mordant mistaken-identity melodrama of *Vertigo*. In *Sisters*, guilt over living when her Siamese twin died, has fractured Margot Kidder's personality into both Danielle and Dominique. In *Phantom Of The Paradise*, William Finley is scarred for life and withdraws into the guise of The Phantom. In *Obsession*, Cliff Robertson courts the image of his lost wife, only to find that she is in fact his daughter. In *Dressed To Kill*, Michael Caine plays a psychologist by day and a psycho-sexual sociopath by night. In *Raising Cain*, John Lithgow was systematically traumatised by his scientist father into developing multiple personalities.

There have been several strands to De Palma's career, several strings of pearls, several personalities at the switch. Firstly there was the radical sixties satirist, then the maker of sophisticated Hitchcockian thrillers through the seventies and into the eighties. Later came the dalliances with respectability and the mainstream which brought forth the gangster epics *Scarface*, *The Untouchables*, and *Carlito's Way*, the alleged comedies *Wise Guys* and *Bonfire Of The Vanities,* the Vietnam crime drama *Casualties Of War* and the big dumb blockbusters *Mission:Impossible* and *Mission To Mars*.

These films range from jobs he did purely to stay in work - *Wise Guys* and *Bonfire* for example - to one of his most personal and heart-felt works - *Casualties Of War* - the box-office failure of which almost destroyed him emotionally.

Throughout these films, the thematic undercurrents of his thrillers are still there, though buried deeper than usual. The theme of suppressed duality is at its most subtle in the place you least expect to find it - in *Scarface*. Pacino's deeply-buried love for his own sister, and for his best and only friend Manny, finally manifests itself as self-destructive psychotic jealousy, with him brutally and impulsively executing Manny mere hours after refusing to blow up a car full of children because it was unethical. Montana (Pacino) is a virulent disease, fatal to all who contract it.

In *The Untouchables* violence is also a disease, a social disease, spread by another Scarface - Robert De Niro's Al Capone. Kevin Costner, under the tutelage of his surrogate father Sean Connery, is transformed by the disease from the clean cut upstanding man who saw wrong and knew how to right it, to a soldier who ".. violated every law I have sworn to uphold, I have become what I beheld and I believe I have done right." He has been absorbed into The Chicago Way. The transformation is painful and permanent.

In *Bonfire Of The Vanities*, Tom Hanks' Sherman McCoy is transformed from a showy, arrogant success to a lowlife disaster, drowning in his own ignorance. He is dragged from the polished granite penthouses of Manhattan to the desolation of Brooklyn by being involved in an accident when out with his mistress. Being of low moral integrity is the key to success on Wall St, but on most other streets it is not a way to make friends. The duality of these characters, the dilemma they must fight through, is the opposition between Integrity and Success. The message of these movies is simple and clear - transformation is painful but essential.

Slowly, torturously, the realisation must have dawned on De Palma that no one was interested in perpetual reruns of fifties thrillers. No one shared his fascination with visual grammar of suspense and action. If he wanted to enjoy the accolades and financial achievements of his contemporaries, he had to put away childish things.

Raising Cain was De Palma's last word (thus far) on his great love. It is replete with references to his own previous references to Hitchcock, as well as drawing on the other great paean to voyeurism and manipulation: Michael Powell's *Peeping Tom*. As Carter Nix, John Lithgow, who has been an easily-overlooked but constant collaborator with De Palma over the years, not only contains the personalities of himself and his brother, but at least two other characters. As the trauma develops, he assumes the identity of Margo and becomes a homicidal woman. When he needs to hide a body, he locks it into a car which he sinks into a lake. It is, for all the world, the coda to De Palma's Hitchcockian Period, his way of saying goodbye to his obsessions. He was clearing the decks so that he could make a concerted effort at achieving the mainstream blockbuster which had always eluded him.

And so we have *Mission:Impossible* and *Mission To Mars*, as obvious and visceral as summer movies could hope to be, with *M:I* earning more money than any other film bearing De Palma's name.

He has achieved his goal and earned the kind of money that all his old friends (save Scorsese - who never makes money, but no one seems to mind) have long been accustomed to. Certainly *M:I* contains moments that are ubiquitous De Palma. The shorthand grammar for a multiple or transformative personalities is no longer the split-screen, but the computer generated morph - as when Jon Voight tears off his face to reveal Tom Cruise beneath.

Long, revealing shots are no longer a conundrum to be solved with intelligence and expertise when you can let the computer blend the edits together so they can't be seen. Computer effects and star names are the currency of big-budget movies. Scripts are prepared methodically and minutely, not as a step to creating something intellectually challenging, but because there can be no room for unnecessary shooting when your star is being paid $20 million for 12 weeks work.

Characters are still ciphers, but their significance is not decided upon in the director's mind - that is the responsibility of financiers' board meetings. The director is not the one in control - that is now the task of a phalanx of producers. In these post-*Star Wars*, post-*Titanic* days, riches beyond the dreams of avarice can be won, providing the product conforms to the pre-set pattern. De Palma is now part of this machine.

De Palma's outlook is unremittingly bleak. He sees the fate of the artist as a choice between being absorbed or being rejected: "Look at Welles, he (was) the greatest director in the world and he (couldn't) get a job and he sold out. Orson Welles on the Johnny Carson show doesn't give us much to hope for. That is the story of this business. It's right there for you to see. Beware. Be aware of what you're getting into."[1]

In the mighty battle between Integrity and Success over the soul of Brian De Palma, Success has won. For now.

Ever the pessimist, De Palma must be writhing in agony at the cost of his new-found respectability: "The problem is that by even dealing with the devil, you become devilish to a certain extent. You need the machine. And once you use it you are a tainted human being."[1]

Quotes:
1: De Palma quoted in *The Movie Brats* by Michael Pye & Lynda Myles. Faber And Faber, 1979.
2: *The Devil's Candy* by Julie Salamon, Jonathan Cape 1991.

3: De Palma quoted in *Out Of The Ashes* by Peter Keough in *Sight And Sound* Vol. 2, No 8, 1992.

4: De Palma quoted in The Bonfire Of The Vanities edition of *The South Bank Show*, 1990.

About This Book

What follows is a list of examples, dealing with all the major themes, motifs and techniques as I see them, on a film-by-film basis. Look upon this volume as a guide book, a road-map to the complex labyrinth of Brian De Palma's imagination.

In some cases I have inevitably indulged in what the Internet would have us dub 'spoilers.' I have tried to avoid this if at all possible but, in many cases, the tricks in the tails of De Palma's films are the points from which all else extends. To ignore the ending would be to miss the point of the film.

With rare exceptions, De Palma's films benefit from repeated viewing. Glance through this book before embarking on one such repeat viewing and, if I have done my job at all adequately, the film will open up before you like a solved Chinese puzzle-box.

I believe most of what I have written is fairly self-explanatory, with the possible exception of my 'Artometer' rating system: In view of my argument that De Palma's career charts a path along an axis from Integrity to Success, I have decided to rate the films accordingly, rather than simply marking them 1 to 5, good to bad, I have decided to rate them as follows:

5/5: An artistic triumph, made without compromise or an eye to box-office revenue.

4/5: An attempt at an artistic statement which didn't quite come off.

3/5: A perfect balance between artistic concerns and commercial concerns. A film which is both good *and* successful.

2/5: An attempt to abandon artistic considerations and make a film purely for the money, which then failed to satisfy.

1/5: A film which succeeded in making money, by sacrificing almost all vestiges of artistic content.

Beyond that, it merely falls to me to mention the superscript numbers you will see in the cast and crew credits. These indicate the number of films that individual has made, up to that point, with De Palma. So, in *Phantom Of The Paradise*, you will find William Finley[5] because this is the fifth De Palma film in which Finley has featured. Names without numbers are of people who have, at least so far, only worked with De Palma the once.

And so you are now ready to begin to cast light into the obscure corners of the dark and dangerous world of Brian De Palma...

The Sixties: Be Black, Baby.

Icarus (1960)

Your usual definition of the term 'short film' involves something of 5 or 10 minutes in length. De Palma obviously doesn't think like this. In his sophomore (second) year at Columbia University, he joined the Columbia Players theatre troupe, but they wouldn't let undergraduates direct, so he went off and looked at making films. Because of his scientific background, he elected to become cameraman. He bought a 16mm Bolex for $150. Later, his director stormed off-set, which left De Palma with no choice but to take over. The result became a self-financed 40-minute 'short.' He now considers *Icarus* to be "pretentious and disastrous but, nonetheless, a beginning."

660124, The Story Of An IBM Card (1961)

This is the story of a painter who sacrifices his life for his art. De Palma sacrificed all the scientific equipment he won at the science fairs of his youth. He financed *660124* with that money and the $500 allowance from his parents. De Palma's opinion of this film is not much higher than of his first: "Pretentious, but a little better, technically."

Wotan's Wake (1962)

This concerns a manic artist, called Wotan, played by William Finley, who falls in love with one of his own sculptures. The statue transforms into a real woman and runs away, with Wotan in hot pursuit. Shot in silent black and white and running some 28 minutes, the film is full of silent comedy references, as well as nods to films as varied as *King Kong* and even Ingmar Bergman's *The Seventh Seal*. Pauline Kael (who remains De Palma's favourite critic) was enthusiastic about *Wotan's Wake*, which went on to win the Rosenthal Foundation Award of $1,000.

The Wedding Party (1964–66, Released 1969)

The Cast: Charles Pfluger (Charlie), Jill Clayburgh (Josephine Fish), William Finley[1] (Alistair), Robert Denero (aka Robert De Niro[1]) (Cecil), John Braswell (Reverend Oldfield), Judy Thomas (Celeste), Jennifer Salt[1] (Phoebe), John Quinn (Baker), Andra Akers[1] (Wedding Guest), Jared Martin[1] (Wedding Guest)

The Crew: Director: Brian De Palma, Writers & Producers: Brian De Palma & Wilford Leach & Cynthia Munroe, Composer: John Herbert McDowell,[1] Cinematographer: Peter Powell, Editor: Brian De Palma

The Plot: Charlie goes to visit his fiancée Josephine in her family home. This is a well-appointed pile amidst rolling countryside, filled with curious characters. Charlie brings his eccentric friends Alistair and Cecil with him, and they fit right in. The narrative then jumps from incident to incident, all loosely connected by this framework of a weekend with weirdos in the wilderness.

The Thickening: Wotan's Wake had won De Palma an MCA writing fellowship, to gain a Masters in Fine Art at his old undergraduate college of Sarah Lawrence, where he had studied acting. He became involved in writing movies scripts. Collaborating with one of the college's acting coaches, Wilford Leach, and attracting the interest of an extremely rich fellow student, Cynthia Munroe (who put up the $100,000 budget), De Palma found himself directing his first 35mm film. It was shot over the summer of 1964, and was then edited over the next 2 years.

Many of the techniques De Palma was to spend the next 3 decades re-using and perfecting are to be found here. Given the naïveté of all concerned, it is a remarkably sure-footed achievement.

The Themes. Voyeurism/Surveillance - Josephine's relatives constantly spy and eavesdrop on the young lovers whenever they attempt to steal any time for themselves.

The Techniques. Slow/Fast-Mo: The opening sequence is an extended shot of a ferry arriving, with Charlie and friends disembarking and being picked up. This is then followed by a madcap sequence with far too many people and possessions crammed into an old-style black soft-top Ford. All of this was shot at 16 frames per second, then played back at 24 fps. This creates the traditional look of silent films, where everyone has that slightly accelerated gait – as exemplified by Charlie Chaplin. Later, when Alistair and Cecil chase the fleeing Charlie, they do so at the Keystone Kop speed of 16fps. He clambers into a rowboat, sets off and finds it sinking under him – a classic silent-movie slapstick routine! After the frenetic opening moments, Charlie meets his beloved's relatives in extended slow motion. (Sometimes, meeting relatives can seem to last forever.) Clearly already benefiting from the influence of the French New Wave and such non-linear directors as Jean-Luc Godard, De Palma fractures the tedious and repetitive scenes of meeting and greeting, by simply jump-cutting without inserting the traditional cutaways.

Stories Within Stories: As The Reverend takes Josephine on a ramble through the woods to tell her an allegorical tale about morality and piety, Charlie rides off and encounters a crowd of bikini-clad girls whose car won't start. You know, like you do. In this rarefied old-world setting, they are a stab of modern, urban, sixties America, completely out of their element. Charlie helps them get their vehicle started, then returns to the main narrative before The Reverend notices he was ever gone.

Split-Screen: Charlie fantasises about the problems of marriage, through superimposed think-bubbles which appear over his head. This allows 2 parallel narratives to occupy the screen at the same time, something De Palma will become increasingly interested in as the years go by.

Long Takes/Tracking Shots: The film's opening shot is a long static shot from some considerable distance, of a ferry arriving. Even sped-up, the shot is notably long. There are many extended dialogue scenes which are almost all shot as single takes. Whether or not this was a stylistic conceit of one forced upon De Palma by lack of time, it is extremely effective. Scenes such as, Alistair and Cecil leaning on a gate in the middle of a field persuading Charlie not to have cold feet; or Charlie, at his reception, working his way up to chatting to the party wallflower, Celeste, show these young actors at their best. Being more accustomed to the stage than the screen, and doubtless as comfortable with improvisation as with scripted dialogue, De Palma's actors probably relished the opportunity to let rip for such extended takes. Finally, the culmination of the weekend of festivities, is the wedding itself, which De Palma introduces emphatically with a long and undoubtedly complicated tracking shot which follows The Reverend as he walks from his house, meeting up with his congregation and leading them to church. The shot gives the impression of having been shot through the side-window of a car, which would certainly be a sensible way of achieving such a monumentally long shot without laying down hundreds of yards of dolly track. Most definitely a taste of things to come!

References: Although there is nothing specifically lifted, the portmanteau structure and silent-movie sequences carry the air of a madcap Frank

Tashlin/Jerry Lewis comedy, such as *Cinderfella* (1960) or *The Disorderly Orderly* (1964).

When Alistair and Cecil take Charlie for a long pre-marital pep talk, they weave back and forth between trees, in a shot which became famous when De Palma re-used it in the early sequence in *Carrie*, where Carrie walks home and is taunted by the boy on the push-bike.

It is at this point that they discuss with Charlie something with which De Palma himself clearly agrees: "Every great man knows how to suffer. Bergman knows how to suffer. Fellini knows how to suffer. Even Hitchcock knows how to suffer." It was really quite daring to mention Hitchcock in such illustrious company back in the mid-sixties, when he was far less lauded than now.

Later, when Charlie and Josephine do finally get some time alone, the camera peeks in at them through a rain-lashed window. We will see further rain-lashed windows throughout De Palma's work, from *Phantom Of The Paradise* to *Bonfire Of The Vanities* to name but 2. I believe these all stem from the shot in *Citizen Kane* (1940) where (with the aid of an edit masked behind a flash of lightning) the camera passes through a closed window, from the tumult outside to the calm of a sleazy bar within.

Eventually it all becomes too much for Charlie and he makes a break for freedom – waiting at a lonely crossroads for a lift. Although this sequence isn't filmed in any way like Hitchcock's classic crop dusting sequence in *North By Northwest* (1959), I suspect that this is what De Palma had in his mind.

Artometer: 4/5

During the extensive breaks in the production of *The Wedding Party*, De Palma made a living directing a few more shorts:

Jennifer (1964)

A filmic portrait of the actress Jennifer Salt who, alongside William Finley, Robert De Niro and Gerrit Graham, would go on to become part of De Palma's regular on-screen ensemble. I'm not sure if it is significant but, as De Palma's career has developed, his most frequent collaborators have shifted from being in front of to being behind the camera – particularly his directors of photography and editors.

Mod (1964)

A documentary appreciation of The Who and The Rolling Stones. This was originally intended to serve as part of a feature-length documentary which was never completed.

Bridge That Gap (1965)

Sponsored by the National Association For The Advancement Of Coloured People (NAACP), this documentary was shot in New Orleans and throughout the South. It made De Palma very aware of black politics in America and would therefore, be a key influence on the creation of the 'Be Black, Baby' section of *Hi Mom!*

You Show Me A Strong Town And I'll Show You A Strong Bank (1966)

As the title suggests, this was a piece of corporate propaganda, made for the Treasury Department. Appropriately, it was a job he did for the money, and it paid him well enough to make ends meet during the interminable post-production process of *The Wedding Party*.

The Responsive Eye (1966)

This was a documentary he made to commemorate the opening of the Kino Art exhibition at The Museum Of Modern Art in New York. Shot in just 4 hours, De Palma decided to film the reactions of the attending aesthetes, rather than show the art itself. This is an idea he would return to when shooting the stage-play *Dionysus In '69*.

These latter 2 paid De Palma enough to begin work on *Murder À La Mod* in collaboration with his college roommates, Jared Martin and Ken Burrows:

Murder À La Mod (1968)

The Cast: Margo Norton (Karen), Andra Akers[2] (Tracy), William Finley[2] (Otto), Jared Martin[2] (Christopher), Jennifer Salt[2] (First Actress), Laura Rubin (Second actress), Melanie Mander (Mannequin), Ken Burrows (Wiley)

The Crew: Writer/Director: Brian De Palma, Producer: Ken Burrows, Cinematographers: Bruce Torbet & Jack Harrell, Editor: Brian De Palma,

Composer: John Herbert McDowell,[2] Song: *Murder À La Mod* written & performed by William Finley

The Plot: Building on the idea Akira Kurosawa had used in *Rashomon* in 1951 and Stanley Kubrick in *The Killing* in 1956 (and since re-visited by *Go!* in 1999), this tells of the same violent incident in three different ways. De Palma's approach is different because he doesn't look at the incident from 3 different perspectives, but presents the same story in 3 stylistically different ways.

The story is about how actress Margo was repeatedly stabbed in the eyes with an ice-pick. The first time we see the story, it is presented like a traditionally bland soap opera. The next version is De Palma's first experiment with Hitchcockian techniques for creating unease. The third is a darkly comic silent movie, with De Palma's then muse, William Finley, playing a deaf-mute actor from whose POV the scene is seen. The idea was, seemingly, to demonstrate how the same horrible event can be manipulated and turned from horror into comedy, purely by changes in its presentation.

The Thickening: This film was not released, it escaped! *Murder À La Mod* ran for 2 weeks in the Gate Theatre in New York's East Village, on a double-bill with Paul Bartel's *Secret Cinema* (1965), a film which, curiously, bears more than a passing resemblance to Peter Weir's *The Truman Show* (1998). After this brief exposure, *Murder À La Mod* disappeared into De Palma's personal archive, perhaps never to be seen again.

De Palma thinks that his script made the film confusing and too shallow. The deliberate artifice of the idea actually worked against it. De Palma was beginning to learn about creating drama using visual grammar.

Since the film, in common with his shorts, hasn't played in public from that day to this, little more is known about it. Time to start a letter writing campaign, I feel. A DVD of De Palma's lost classics would go down very nicely thank-you!

Artometer: 4/5

Greetings (1968)

The Cast: Jonathan Warden (Paul Shaw), Robert De Niro[2] (Jon Rubin), Gerrit Graham[1] (Lloyd Clay), Allen Garfield[1] (aka Alan Garfield) (Smut Peddler)

The Crew: Director: Brian De Palma, Writers: Brian De Palma & Charles Hirsch,[1] Cinematographer: Robert Fiore, Editor: Brian De Palma, Composers: Eric Kaz[1] & J Stephen Soles & Artie Traum

The Plot: This film basically tells of a week in the lives of 3 reasonably average teenagers in the late sixties. Paul has received his Vietnam call-up papers and is desperately trying to think of ways of failing the medical. Lloyd is obsessed with unravelling the conspiracies surrounding the Kennedy assassination. Jon, by contrast, is developing his hobby of being a peeping tom. Ahh, America's youth. Their mothers would be so proud!

The Thickening: Whilst most people of his generation were supposedly turning on, tuning in and, if truth be known, dropping off; De Palma was putting it all down on film. *Greetings* and its sequel *Hi Mom!* are almost unique in that their satirical critique of the politically compromised, culturally confused years of the late sixties, was conceived at ground zero. These aren't revisionist movies looking back at a decade of decadence, they were conceived, written and made by the people who were living the lie at the time. Much as they made fun of it, De Palma's cast were genuinely terrified of being called-up to die in Vietnam.

It seems that De Palma's main concern here, was an exploration of the invasiveness of the various forms of photography and film-making, looking at how corrupting and distracting they can be. Since the entire movie was shot in just 2 weeks, for $40,000, his achievement is quite extraordinary.

The Themes. Sexism: If De Palma were a European film-maker, the images of women with which he is happy to fill his films would probably pass without undue comment. But he isn't. He's American, and the exploitation of the female form carries very different political and social weight there.

It might be worth mentioning, at this point, that I consider Antonioni's *Blow-Up* (1966) to be a shockingly misogynistic film, irrespective of its country of origin. David Hemmings, the photographer in that film, displays a complete inability to perceive his female models as human beings. Since it remains De Palma's favourite film of the period, he borrows many of *Blow-Up*'s themes and concerns, including its shameful attitude towards women. The closest I can come to justifying this is to note that such disregard for the rights and opinions of women was commonplace at the time.

If the documentary evidence from the time is to be believed, women genuinely thought that 'free love' was for their benefit. It was only when they started falling pregnant or catching diseases that they began to realise that the men were having a wail of a time at their expense. I think it was Fay Weldon who said that women knew their place in the sixties - it was on their backs with their legs in the air. When Jon goes to see a female photographer, she redresses the film's sexist imbalance somewhat, by undressing him and treating him with all the respect he has reserved for so many women.

Voyeurism/Surveillance: Lloyd secretly watches a photographer seducing one of his models – this is just one of the many direct references to *Blow-Up*. There is also much consideration of surveillance as a form of voyeurism here – such as in Lloyd's obsessive poring over the photographs of the Kennedy killing. He also talks about the police bugging Lee Harvey Oswald's phone.

When Lloyd is discussing the Kennedy assassination with the panicky 'witness' in the bookshop, the entire conversation is witnessed by an eavesdropping Jon. They are paranoid about being overheard, yet fail to notice Jon.

This act of eavesdropping, seems to put Jon on the path to becoming a 'peeper.' His heart's desire becomes the spurious concept of 'peep art' where he gets to watch and photograph women undressing. This will go on to become an obsession for him. At a party, he sees a striking blonde woman, and feels compelled to follow her. This will become the first of many unsubtle pursuits De Palma will put on film over the next 30 years. As Jon waits outside an art gallery watching his prey, he attracts the attention of a pornographer, who sells him some street corner smut and, did he but know it, lays the foundations for the sequel, *Hi Mom!*

The Techniques. POV: When no one else will listen to Lloyd about his batty conspiracy theories, he starts addressing them directly to us, the viewer. Later, it seems like he is groping a naked woman, until we realise he is using her as a canvass on which to draw. Then, to implicate us in this abuse of her, he looks straight at the camera and begins another of his lectures. Jon reads an extract from a book on sexual deviancy to us. It charts the subject's incestuous sexual frustration and ends simply: "He began peeping regularly." This plants the seed of an idea in Jon's head. When he has persuaded Linda to allow him to film her undressing, we see the entire sequence from the perspective of his camera. At one point the screen goes blank because his film has run out. At a party, in the foreground a seasoned Vietnam vet is growling on about his experiences, yet he is completely out of focus – our attention being drawn to the stunning blonde who enters. This demonstrates where the typical male gaze settles whenever a beautiful woman enters the room. In this case the male in question is Jon. When Jon is out in 'Nam, we see him from the perspective of a documentary film camera. He notices a local girl. She is the first woman he has seen since leaving the States. His first thought is to start using the documentary camera the way he has been using his own – to peep.

Slow/Fast-Mo: When Jon watches the porno film he has bought, it is a speeded-up 'What the butler saw' type of silent film.

Stories Within Stories: This tale begins and ends with a close-up of a television screen, reporting on events in Vietnam. Johnson is holding forth about how 'we' will sacrifice to maintain The American Dream. By 'we' he, of course, means 'you.' At the end, he opines "I don't wanna say 'You've never had it so good!' But it's true, isn't it!?" Well, that rather depends on your perspective. After Jon wings it through his draft board, he suddenly appears within a documentary film-in-film, as a soldier out in 'Nam.

Split-Screen: Although there are no examples of the screen actually being divided in half with two pictures, there are several examples of a different form of split-screen which, if anything, De Palma practices with greater frequency than the commonly-understood form. Comparing the foreground action to the background action offers a sort of 3-dimensional split-screen where, very often, the background relates directly to, or contrasts deliberately with, the foreground. In his later, bigger-budgeted films, De Palma achieved this through the use of split-dioptre lenses, which allow two planes of focus – one in the extreme background, one in the extreme foreground. For example, during an early scene, in the background of the shot Lloyd and Jon are persuading Paul there are any number of ways of avoiding the draft, whilst customers come and go and business carries on in the foreground. While Lloyd sits in the extreme foreground discussing a street artist's work with him, Jon and Paul romp around in the background, trying to stay awake after a day of running around. As Jon is desperately trying to persuade Linda of the validity of his need to watch her take her clothes off, he describes a 'for instance' scenario. Whilst he does this, a window lights up behind him and, unseen by either him or Linda, the scene he is describing is acted out.

Long Takes/Tracking Shots: The opening credits roll over a hand-held tracking shot, following Paul as he walks nervously down a street, then into a bar to get beaten up. He will do anything to avoid passing his military medical. Paul goes on an unsuccessful computer date with a secretary, which is seen in one shot. When Lloyd acts out his theory about the bullet entering Kennedy's body, by painting red lines on a naked girl, we see it in one sustained shot.

References: As with *The Wedding Party*, the different tableaux are separated by introductory inter-titles, as in silent movies. When Lloyd and

Jon are force-marching Paul to make him tired, they weave in and out of concrete pillars. This shot involved an avenue of trees when De Palma previously used it in *The Wedding Party*, and he subsequently used it in *Carrie*. Lloyd mentions the film *Blow-Up*, when looking at the street artist's enlarged photos. He, himself, has blow-up photos of the grassy knoll, thereby linking the forensic examination of film, with the conspiracy theories surrounding the Kennedy assassination. When he visits the photo studio, he attempts to impress the girl there with his theories. She replies: "I saw *Blow-Up*, I know how this turns out – you can't see anything!" When Jon is pursuing his blonde dream-girl, he waits for her while she wanders around an art-gallery. A sequence not greatly dissimilar to the art-gallery waltz between Angie Dickinson and her pursuer in *Dressed To Kill*. The speeded up porno film which Jon watches, not only alludes to the silent films so beloved of De Palma, it also pre-empts Kubrick's fast-forward shag-fest in *Clockwork Orange* (1971)! Lloyd finally gets his wish – he is sucked into a Kennedy conspiracy. In De Palma's first overtly Hitchcockian moment – Lloyd is shot dead in a public place. The final scene of Jon exploiting the Vietnamese girl, are an eerie precursor of *Casualties Of War*, although the true incidents which inspired that film weren't reported until the year after *Greetings* was made. This proximity might explain why the story made such an impact on De Palma and wouldn't leave him alone until he filmed it 20 years later.

Artometer: 5/5

Hi, Mom! (1969)

The Cast: Robert De Niro[3] (Jon Rubin), Gerrit Graham[2] (Gerrit Wood), Jennifer Salt[3] (Judy Bishop), Allen Garfield[2] (Joe Banner), Charles Durnham (aka Charles Durning[1]) (Superintendent), Paul Bartel (Uncle Tom Wood – allegedly, but you try and spot him, 'cos no one I know can)

The Crew: Director: Brian De Palma, Writers: Brian De Palma & Charles Hirsch,[2] Producer: Charles Hirsch, Composer: Eric Kaz,[2] Cinematographer: Robert Elfstrom, Editor: Paul Hirsch,[1]

The Plot: Following on from *Greetings*, this tale tells of Jon Rubin's return from Vietnam to an America no less confused and compromised than the one he left. His obsession with peeping has become a career because he works for the smut peddler he met in *Greetings*, filming the activities of the denizens of the housing project opposite his apartment. Gradually he is drawn into radical politics by a theatre troupe and their spurious campaign to get white people to sympathise with black people, by simply reversing roles. By the film's end, he has learned nothing, has contributed little and his only achievement is actually staying alive. I wonder what he's up to these days?

The Thickening: This film cements once and for all a theme which reappears throughout De Palma's canon – the exploration of the effects of filming and being filmed, of watching and being watched. Almost all of the characters here are making films or being filmed. *Hi Mom!* lacks the spontaneity or, to be honest, the energy of *Greetings*, but it is far more sophisticated. This was a by-product of the doubling of the budget to $95,000 and the corresponding doubling of the shooting schedule to a positively roomy 4 weeks.

The Themes. Voyeurism/Surveillance: He knows that there are 270 windows in the building opposite his, and he has decided on the 6 windows which are 'the most interesting.' These generally feature single males or females who entertain members of the opposite sex. Curiously, they also have cameras on tripods in their windows, implying that what Jon is doing is far from unique. Clearly, his peeping desires are motivated by his fear of getting too close – literally. However, he very quickly becomes frustrated with this distance, so arranges to introduce himself into his own dramas, seducing his subjects and (he hopes) catching it all on film. His desire is changing from watching to being watched. When he is in his chosen victim's room, pretending to use her phone (whilst really checking light levels) his role has been reversed on him – he is being eavesdropped upon by his supposed prey.

The Motifs. Colours: De Palma's pointed playing with colour begins here. Gerrit believes that 'being black' is all a matter of skin colour and therefore, if he paints himself black he will indeed be black, baby. This is taken to its illogical extreme by his political theatre troupe and the films they make under the banner of NIT - National Intellectual Television. The highly charged and deeply disturbing 'Be Black, Baby' segment is a black and white documentary of the guilty white middle classes being painted black and abused by black men and women who are painted white. A ridiculously simplistic reduction of sixties racial politics, which seems all the tougher, when you remember that De Palma was making this satire about his world as he saw it at that time – not as some safely abstracted past.

Masks/Multiple Personas: To avenge the death of all his 'friends,' Jon hatches a plot to assume the role of an unassuming, mild-mannered insurance salesman. Addicted to his fantasies, he immerses himself so completely in this role that he stays under cover for 3 months. In this relatively short space of time, he finds an apartment, a wife and all the shackles of normality. Then he drops his pretence and blows up the entire building, with everyone in it – including his wife. Were it not for the fact that it were at the beginning of his career, one could almost see this as De Niro satirising his own subsequent method-actor mania for completely immersing himself in his characters.

The Techniques. POV: The film begins with an extended sequence shot from Jon's point of view as he investigates the delights of the worst rented apartment on earth. In the camera shop, Jon is seen from the perspective of one of the cameras.

After the 'Be Black, Baby' sequence, the NIT-wits choose to participate in more direct action against the bloated, white middle classes. They attack one of their housing tenements and the camera goes along. At one point, Gerrit points his gun directly at us, the bloated, white middle-class intellectuals who watch this sort of film. After all the NITs pomposity and petty-minded cruelty, it is a delight to find that the bloated, white middle classes are armed and waiting.

Slow/Fast-Mo: When Jon takes his idea of pornographic 'peep art' to 'The Contemporary American Film Salon,' he arrives at the accelerated pace of the porno film he watched in *Greetings*. Similarly, when he is showing Banner, the smut dealer, what he can see through his neighbours' windows – by using a telescope – the view through the scope is speeded up, reminding the viewer, again, of a 'What the Butler Saw' type of film.

Stories Within Stories: As Jon sets himself up to observe his neighbours, the screen divides up, like the title sequence of a sit-com, putting each of his unwitting neighbours in their own little screen-within-screen, pursuing their own little lives.

The most disturbing and memorable sequence in this whole film, is the 17 minute bogus documentary at its heart. The 'Be Black, Baby' movie is shot entirely hand-held and has hardly been edited at all. Its stark, grainy images of seemingly real people really panicking, predate *The Blair Witch Project* by exactly 30 years, yet employ all the same ideas – the improvised dialogue, the dark, alien environment, the lack of clear definition between those who were acting and those who weren't. The most convincing tool De Palma uses, however, is the shaky, imprecise camerawork and lackadaisical approach to editing. All of these things combine, over a length of time, to persuade you to forget you are watching a fictional movie, and draw you in to this apparent truth.

The film finishes with Jon returning to the scene of the bombing and – seen from the perspective of a television camera – he gets to wave at the camera and utter 'Hi, mom!' Twenty films and 29 years later, Rick Santoro will reach the end of his career in *Snake Eyes* with a shrug and a philosophical comment: "At least I got to be on TV." I suppose some things never change.

Split-Screen: While the NIT protesters are busily attacking innocent passers-by about social injustice, unnoticed in the background a newspaper stall is robbed and the owner murdered.

Long Takes/Tracking Shots: Jon's entire life as an undercover insurance salesman is represented by one very long take of domestic tedium.

References: Jon setting up his camera and watching his neighbours is a deliberate reference to Hitchcock's *Rear Window* (1954). Because he has no sound, the narratives he watches from across the street are all silent and presented at the traditional 16fps silent-movie speed. Like *Greetings*, this film is influenced by Antonioni's *Blow-Up* - on his wall Jon has blow-ups of the various rooms in the building opposite. After abandoning his pornographic aspirations and moving into urban terrorism, Jon wears a green army jacket and applies to play the cop in 'Be Black, Baby.' His rehearsal, out in a corridor with a nightstick and a stepladder, is disturbingly close to the trigger-happy madness he would bring to Travis Bickle in *Taxi Driver*.

Artometer: 5/5

The Seventies: Burn In Hell

Dionysus In '69 (1970)

The Cast: The Performance Group: William Finley[3] (Dionysus), William Shephard (Pentheus), Joan MacIntosh (Agave), Samuel Blazer (Coryphee), with Judith Allen, Remi Barclay, Jason Bousseau, Richard Dia, Vickie May, Patrick McDermott, Margaret Ryan and Ciel Smith

The Crew: Directors: Brian De Palma & Robert Fiore & Bruce Rubin, Producers: De Palma & Fiore & Rubin & The Performance Group, Cinematographers: Brian De Palma & Robert Fiore, Editors: Brian De Palma & Bruce Rubin, Director Of Stage Production: Richard Schechner

The Thickening: A black and white cinéma vérité film of an 'environmental theatre' stage performance of *Dionysus In '69* which, in turn, is based on Euripedes' *The Bacchae*. The entire performance was filmed at The Performing Garage in New York.

The film is split-screen throughout. The actors are seen from 2 different perspectives, or with the performance on one side, and the audience's reaction to it on the other. This was the year before *Woodstock* (which uses the same technique extensively) was released.

In 1975, De Palma told *Cinefantastique* magazine: "I was very strongly affected by the play when I saw it. Bill Finley had been playing Dionysus with the group for some time. I came to see him and said, 'God, this is incredible,' environmental theatre, the way it affects the audience and draws them into the piece itself. This was the most exciting thing I'd seen on stage in years. So I began to try and figure out a way to capture it on film. I came up with the idea of split-screen, to be able to show the audience involvement, to trace the life of the audience and that of the play as they merge in and out of each other... I think it will live long, long after some of my other movies."

Unfortunately, since the film hasn't been shown publicly for decades (although it apparently does get the occasional airing for theatre students), I respectfully submit, this is not the way to ensure your films 'live.'

Artometer: 5/5

Get To Know Your Rabbit (1972)

The Cast: Tommy Smothers (Donald Beeman), John Astin (Turnbull), Katharine Ross (Terrific-Looking Girl), Orson Welles (Mr Delasandro), Allen Garfield[3] (Vic), M Emmet Walsh (Wendel)

The Crew: Director: Brian De Palma, Writer: Jordan Crittenden, Composers: Jack Elliott & Allyn Ferguson, Cinematographer: John A Alonzo,[1] Editors: Peter Colbert & Frank J Urioste

The Plot: Sick of working for a large corporation, Donald Beeman quits his job, leaves his wife and sets out to make it big in the world of showbiz. He enrols in a conjuring school run by the enigmatic Mr Delasandro, who presents Beeman and his classmates with rabbits which they are instructed to "get to know."

Beeman graduates from Delasandro's unique college and tries to make a living as a tap-dancing magician on the cabaret circuit. In the meantime, his old boss, Mr Turnbull loses his job and becomes an alcoholic.

Taking pity on his old employer, Beeman hires Turnbull as his agent. Turnbull's capitalistic 'creativity' soon turns Beeman from a tap-dancing magician into a booming business. This is precisely what Beeman was trying to get away from. Determined to escape the corporate rat race once and for all, Beeman uses his magical powers to disappear for good. Given what happened subsequently, it all now seems terribly symbolic of De Palma's Hollywood career.

The Thickening: After the critical success of *Greetings* and *Hi Mom!*, it was only a matter of time before De Palma received his call-up papers from Hollywood. Offered a chance to helm a picture for Warner Brothers, De Palma took one look at the fee and at the cast (which featured his hero Orson Welles) and booked himself on the next flight out of New York.

During the first week of shooting, the young director reportedly banged heads many times with the man who'd made *Citizen Kane*. As soon as they'd marked out their territory, however, De Palma and Welles got on marvellously. The great director/actor/writer/producer/broadcaster/bullfighter obviously saw something of his youthful self in De Palma. Given the repeated humiliations Welles had suffered at the hands of unsympathetic studios, he was going to find they had even more in common by the time the film was released!

Welles gave unstinting support to the 30-year-old De Palma when things started to turn sour. The sourness came courtesy of leading man Tom Smothers. Upset with the tone of De Palma's picture, Smothers whinged to the producers that the director was ruining his shot at big-screen stardom. Smothers, being a big TV star, carried far more clout than a New York know-nothing and a burnt-out old hack, so the studio listened to his complaints and fired De Palma.

Another director was hired to ghost-direct new sequences, whilst a bunch of De Palma's scenes were cut. This new, studio-approved cut of *Get To Know Your Rabbit* debuted in 1972, 2 years after De Palma completed the picture. It died and so did Tommy Smothers' movie career. Shame.

The Themes. Violence: In De Palma's original cut, Beeman registers his disgust with Turnbull by killing a rabbit on prime time television. The sequence is one of the many Warners stripped from the film prior to release.

Voyeurism/Surveillance: Since *Rabbit* is a film largely about the art of performance, voyeurism is no longer a theme but the subject. To be successful, one has to get oneself in front of the television cameras. This particular theme would have been even more overt if De Palma's rabbit-slaughtering sequence survived.

The Motifs. Colours: Employing the saturated colour palette more commonly associated with late sixties television (*The Man From U.N.C.L.E.* springs to mind) De Palma's depiction of the showbiz world is so gaudy, it makes Reno look like Rochdale. Just check out the blue and red handkerchiefs that Beeman's classmates juggle, and the tap-dancing magician's T-shirt that our hero receives in lieu of a graduation certificate.

Artometer: 2/5

(Note: This film was written-up by the noble Richard Luck... cos he's seen it and I haven't yet! He would like the world to know that he watched it purely because he is an aficionado of Welles, and not because of any latent sexual attraction to rabbits. That's a different thing entirely...)

Sisters (1973)

The Cast: Margot Kidder (Danielle Breton), Jennifer Salt[3] (Grace Collier), Charles Durning[2] (Larch), Bill (William) Finley[4] (Dr Emil Breton), Lisle Wilson (Philip Woode), Barnard Hughes (McLennen), Mary Davenport[1] (Mrs Collier), Dolph Sweet (Detective Kelly), Olympia Dukakis (Louise Wolanski, The Woman In The Cake Shop, uncredited)

The Crew: Director: Brian De Palma, Writers: Brian De Palma & Louisa Rose, Producers: Edward R Pressman[1] & Louis A Stroller,[1] Composer: Bernard Herrmann,[1] Cinematographer: Gregory Sandor, Editor: Paul Hirsch[2]

UK Title: Blood Sisters

The Plot: Having been an unwitting contestant on the taste-free game show *Peeping Toms*, where he was tested to see if he would secretly watch a woman undress, Philip Woode asks said woman, part-time actress and model Danielle Breton, out on a date. They have a wonderful time.

Next morning, Philip discovers that it is Danielle and her twin sister, Dominique's birthday. Although he hasn't met Dominique yet, he buys them both a cake, and offers it to Danielle with a big cake knife. She hacks him to death with this. The knife, not the cake.

Her neighbour, journalist Grace Collier, sees Philip dying and calls the police. When they arrive at Danielle's apartment, there is no sign of a struggle. So begins a cat and mouse game as Grace investigates Danielle, her peculiar husband Emil and her mysterious sister, Dominique.

The Thickening: This was De Palma's first attempt at an out and out genre picture. After having his fingers burned with the studio interference on *Rabbit*, he went off by himself again, but decided to put on hold his experiments with The New Wave and dedicate himself, instead, to working with Hitchcock's visual grammar. This is the first De Palma film in which set design, colour palette and music begin to carry serious significance. Although his view of the world is still stylised, it is no longer satirising the world around us but creating detailed and intelligent fictions to divert us.

The Themes. Manipulation: Using drugs and hypnosis, Emil manages to persuade Grace that there was no murder. This suggestion takes root so well that, even when everyone does finally believe her, she no longer believes herself. During her hallucinations, she witnesses Emil's greatest act of cruel manipulation, as he persuades Danielle to allow him to drug Dominique and, eventually, to attempt to separate Danielle from her.

Sexism: The first hint of sexism comes when Danielle has to make a living for herself – by, in essence, taking her clothes off in public. Later, we learn she has an extremely low self-opinion, prompted by her guilt over her part in her sister's fate.

Emil's attitude towards Dominique was every bit as fascist as his slicked-back hair and needle moustache implies. He simply saw her as an inconvenient lump of meat attached to her sister's side, and had her removed so his relations with Danielle could be more comfortable. The fact that his plan backfired is only a shame in that, ultimately, he is the one who suffers the least.

Violence: The first sign of violence we see is with the vaginal gash on Danielle's upper thigh where, we later learn, she was separated from her sister. When she attacks Philip, she stabs him in roughly the same place, attempting to emasculate him. Much later, when she is rebelling against Emil, she grabs a scalpel – the instrument which separated her from her sister and thereby unhinged her mind – and stabs him, once again in the upper thigh.

Voyeurism/Surveillance: The bargain-basement game show *Peeping Toms* sadly predicts the lamentable state of global television some 25 years before *The Truman Show* (1998) and *EdTV* (1999). Nowadays, gawping at poorly-filmed images from other people's private lives is a massive and increasingly popular industry – fuelled by Jennicam and all of her webcam copyists.

When Philip makes it into Danielle's apartment and she absent-mindedly re-enacts her televisual striptease, he doesn't turn his back this time but, having decided he's now on a promise, enjoys every moment.

The character of Larch is something of a throwback to the mischievous comic edge of De Palma's sixties films. He is a slightly officious, far from inspired, private detective. When he is rummaging around in Danielle's house, Grace watches his progress through a pair of binoculars. He is smart enough to realise that the body is in the sofa, then sets about doggedly keeping track of it. He then vanishes from the film, only reappearing as the end credits roll, suspended up a telephone pole, watching the sofa from afar, as if he is expecting it to get up and walk away. He could still be there to this day.

The Motifs. Colours: At Danielle's building, the hallways have red walls, whilst her apartment has stark white walls. As will become increasingly clear with De Palma's films, no good can come to a woman who lives in a white-walled house. Whereas traditional semiotics would ascribe only good intentions to the colour white, De Palma turns that on its head. Bad things happen in white houses, bad guys wear white hats. Evil is almost always enacted under the cover of white.

The all-important sofa bed is white (with a conspicuous red stain on it). When it is transported, it is wrapped in a white sheet. I suppose, given *Hi, Mom!*'s playing around with the concepts of black and white, it ought to be noted that Philip, hidden away in that white sofa, is actually black. Although, by the end of the movie, he's more likely blue!

Doubles: Grace begins to realise that Danielle is hiding someone (or something) when she notices that she has two of everything in her wardrobe. This is because Danielle used to have a double – a twin sister, now dead. She can't accept the guilt of still being alive, so has recreated this double in her own head, and it takes control of her body from time to time

Masks/Multiple Personas: After a night of passion, Danielle withdraws into Dominique's room and seemingly talks to her. As with Norman Bates, this is just her externalising her guilt. When she is caught breaking in to Emil's asylum, he spontaneously gives her a new name and creates a whole new identity for her – as a deluded patient desperately in need of his drugs. Later, after her dose of hypnosis, she has changed. Her mother comments, ruefully, "She's just not quite herself."

The Techniques. POV: In a successful attempt to avoid the trap into which *Psycho* fell – of having a psychologist standing and explaining what had happened in Norman's past – De Palma opts to use extensive POV hallucinations. Grace imagines herself as Dominique, being drugged, betrayed and eventually murdered by her conniving sister and her lover, Emil. When Emil hypnotises Grace, to increase the sense of violation which should accompany such a betrayal of trust by a doctor, De Palma opts to put us in Grace's place.

Stories Within Stories: Grace first learns the story behind The Blanchion Twins by being shown an old documentary film (no newspaper cuttings for De Palma, he prefers his images moving!) McLennen, the journalist who introduces this film to her, gives the speech which De Palma himself would probably best identify with: "To me, at any rate, the psychological and philosophical elements are of extreme importance." The film within the film then shows how Danielle and Dominique grew up under Emil's supervision.

Split-Screen: The first split-screen sequence features Philip dying inside the house, whilst Grace sees him through the window from across the road. This continues with Emil's arrival and frenzied attempts to clean up the mess. For 9 long minutes this sequence continues, as Emil and Danielle hide the body inside the sofa bed on which she had just had sex. Downstairs, Grace bickers with the police who refuse to rush. Both narratives climax with the police's eventual arrival at Danielle's door. They stand in the red corridor, in their black suits, whilst she wears a pink silk gown which shines with the stark white of the walls around her.

Long Takes/Tracking Shots: Grace's lengthy and clearly oft-repeated argument with her mother (played by Mary Davenport, Jennifer Salt's real mother) about her 'little job,' is one long sustained shot.

References: No movie since *Psycho* (1960) had really gone for shocks and violence in quite the way *Sisters* does. In acknowledgement of this, De Palma mirrors *Psycho*'s unique and clearly identifiable narrative. The first half-hour or so follows one character until we identify with them and accept that the film will be about them. Then they are suddenly, brutally murdered and the narrative undergoes a massive paradigm shift as it becomes a murder mystery with a woman investigating the murder when the police refuse to. The villain, it transpires, has a multiple personality, and therefore doesn't even know that they did it.

At the moment *Sisters* turns from love story to horror story – Bernard Herrmann kicks in with a reworking of his discordant *Psycho* strings, and the camera cuts to the shadow of a huge knife, hacking away. As Philip crawls across the floor, leaving a smear of blood behind him, we are seeing the first of De Palma's messy, protracted death scenes, which reach their zenith with Sean Connery in *The Untouchables*.

Grace's lengthy POV hallucination, was inspired by Mia Farrow's similar hallucinations of her demonic rape in Roman Polanski's *Rosemary's Baby* (1968).

The birthmark on Emil's forehead is not dissimilar to the birthmark De Palma's much-resented elder brother Bruce had over one eye. Since Emil is the first truly evil character in De Palma's canon, this would imply that even in adulthood the 2 brothers failed to patch up their differences.

Artometer: 5/5

Phantom Of The Paradise (1974)

The Cast: William Finley[5] (Winslow Leach), Paul Williams (Swan), Jessica Harper (Phoenix), Gerrit Graham[3] (Beef), Harold Oblong, Jeffrey Comanor & Archie Hahn (The Juicy Fruits/The Beach Bums/The Undeads), Rod Serling (Narrator, uncredited)

The Crew: Writer/Director: Brian De Palma, Producer: Edward R Pressman,[2] Composer: George Aliceson Tipton, Songs: Paul Williams, Cinematographer: Larry Pizer, Editor: Paul Hirsch[3]

Working Title: Phantom

The Plot: Faust meets *The Phantom of the Opera* in seventies pop music spectacular! A mysterious impresario, Swan, steals the music of struggling composer Winslow Leach and has Leach thrown in prison. Winslow escapes and attempts to destroy Swan's record-pressing plant but is disfigured and left for dead.

But he re-emerges as The Phantom – determined to terrorise all who work at Swan's new theatre, The Paradise. Eventually, Winslow signs an exclusive contract with the devilish Swan, on the understanding that all his work will be sung by Phoenix, the woman he loves but to whom he can now never show his true face.

Of course, The Devil rarely keeps his side of the bargain.

The Thickening: Pre-dating *The Rocky Horror Show*, and the pomp-rock of Kiss, this is the culmination of the early, eclectic phase of De Palma's career. He has never since wandered quite so far from the expected path. He has also never again tried his hand at the musical form, which is a shame, because we could do with more live-action musicals with teeth!

Here, De Palma's merciless gaze uses the old *Phantom Of The Opera* tale to make some swingeing observations about the seventies music industry – criticisms which are even more cutting in the post-Spice Girls feeding frenzy. Swan runs his empire with an iron hand – all of his performers are objects to be moulded to his will, whether through use of sex, threats or drugs.

De Palma's opinion of all this and, for that matter, of the big-budget film industry as well, would seem to be captured in Philbin's complaint about the continued success of form over content: "No one cares what anything's about!" To prove this, at the end, when the artist and the impresario lie dead, the kids just keep on dancing.

The Themes. Violence: In keeping with the slapstick presentation of Winslow's incarceration, the violence visited upon him is of a cartoonish, if gruesome, nature: He has his teeth forcibly extracted, and then has his face mashed in a record-press. Beef's death by electrocution is similarly camp in its execution. The real violence here, is in Swan's abuse of his power over the young and naïve.

Voyeurism/Surveillance: Swan's main hobby seems to be surveillance. He has cameras in all the changing rooms of The Paradise, so he can watch his subjects (like when Beef is in the shower) and replays the tapes to amuse himself. He also must replay the tape of his contract with The Devil, who manifests as his narcissistic reflection. This tape was only made because Swan wanted to record his own suicide for posterity – the culmination of the 'die young stay pretty' mentality which permeated the music industry throughout the sixties and seventies.

When Winslow follows Swan and Phoenix back to his mansion, Swanage, he watches his master lying cruciform on his bed, while Phoenix ministers to him. The scene folds in on itself when we realise that there is a camera behind Winslow, on the rain-lashed roof and, as he watches Swan he is, in turn, being watched by Swan.

The Motifs. Colour: Swan generally wears white – so you know he isn't to be trusted. Yet, to empower him, he is surrounded by red. Red walls. Red bed sheets. When Winslow is completely in Swan's thrall – attempting to secure a moment's audience with him – he disguises himself in a red dress.

Later, when Swan betrays Winslow and steals his life's work, he locks him in a cold, black room at the end of a claustrophobic red corridor. It will become very common in a De Palma film for doorways and corridors to be red – this implies transition. Red is also an empowering colour, so if you have anything important to do in a De Palma film wear red!

Doubles: Swan and Winslow form a binary of opposites – Swan is normal on the outside, yet mutated within, whilst Winslow has a corrupted exterior, but the heart of a poet. The bond between them is symbolised by the masks they must wear. When these masks are torn off, both men are revealed to be grotesque.

Driven to despair, Winslow tries to commit suicide by stabbing himself in his broken heart. Swan simply withdraws the blade: "This contract terminates with Swan." Winslow lunges and plunges – attempting to kill Swan and therefore himself. This also fails because: "I'm under contract too!" So, Swan and Winslow have much in common and now, thanks to that open wound, their fates are inextricably linked. When Swan dies, so will Winslow.

Masks/Multiple Personas: The rock and roll band of the opening number – The Juicy Fruits, becomes The Beach Bums and finally The Undeads. To break into Swan's palace, Winslow dresses up as a girl, then writhes around on his bed with the other girls of the 'audition.' Swan hides behind a mask of Devilish design – a black magic version of the mask Winslow must hide behind.

Throughout, Swan reflects people's gaze, by hiding in the dark or behind mirrors – this is because, if he is photographed the artificial medium will see him as he truly is, not as his Devilish disguise has him appear. Similarly, his microphones record his true garbled voice!

The Techniques. POV: Much of the film is seen from Swan's POV. Philbin, his ever-present acolyte, addresses the film's opening lines to us/ Swan in this manner. This implicates the viewer with the devilish deeds in which Swan indulges. When Winslow is beaten up and thrown out of Swan's castle into the hands of the police, we see then gazing down from his prone POV. Later, in the kind of sequence which has now (through its use in John Carpenter's *Halloween* (1978) and all of that film's copyists) become a staple of the horror genre: Winslow arrives at the Paradise and dons his new mask for the first time. This is all done in an extended tracking shot (with some hidden edits) seen from Winslow's POV. When Phoenix is auditioning for Swan, her gaze swings from him directly to us, the viewer. We don't see her vicariously through the eyes of a character, but one-to-one, she draws us directly into the film.

Slow/Fast-Mo: Winslow's incarceration, escape and final disfigurement are all shot at the silent-movie speed of 16fps, then played back at 24fps. This is accompanied by the traditional silent-movie tacky piano accompaniment.

Stories Within Stories: The film begins with a 'once upon a time' narration, by Rod Serling – in his trademark *Twilight Zone* style. Although there are no flashbacks here, we learn of Swan's past through viewing his recording of his own damnation. Also, Winslow's 'Phoenix Cantata' contains its own internal narrative, which mirrors the tale in which Winslow finds himself trapped. It has the line: "The Devils that disturb me and the Angels that defeated them, somehow."

Split-Screen: As the film opens and Philbin is talking to Swan in the foreground, out of focus and in the extreme background, Winslow makes his entrance, sets up his piano and begins singing. Not a literal split-screen, but one of those 3-dimensional shots De Palma also loves, which employ the full frame and a range of depths of field as narrative tools.

The first sequence of genuine split-screen comes in the form of two interconnecting long takes when The Phantom plants a bomb in The Beach Bums' car. As with the single split-screen sequence in *Bonfire*, we see what is going on out front, and the shenanigans going on backstage, simultaneously, so we can compare the reality to the appearance. This sequence finishes with Swan seeing The Phantom for the first time.

Long Takes/Tracking Shots: The first long take is the 360 rotation around Winslow as he plays his audition song in the film's opening moments. From here on in it is common for De Palma to shoot scenes where people are sitting down but the camera is moving.

The first long take is the previously-discussed scene where Winslow arrives at The Paradise, all seen from his POV, cunningly edited to appear as one long shot when it is, in fact, several. The other notably long takes come with the two halves of the split-screen sequence.

References: Firstly, there is the paradise subtext which runs through De Palma's work. In this case it is the name of the domicile of the devil's plaything, a place fuelled by corruption, exploitation and drugs. The opposite, in other words, of the received definition of paradise. In *Greetings*, the music was performed by The Children Of Paradise. In *Scarface*, we are introduced to Miami through a painted sunset, next to which is a greasy burger bar optimistically named El Paradiso. The nightclub Carlito Brigante takes over is similarly named El Paraiso. This is the place where his dreams of retirement in paradise almost reach fruition.

Throughout *Phantom*, there are references to Hollywood movies of the thirties. The thirties were the first full decade of sound, when there was the first great flourishing of the musical, as often as not in the form of backstage romances. It was also the decade of Grand Guignol horror classics like *Frankenstein* (1931) and gangster movies with their montages and spinning newspaper headlines. All of these genre motifs are represented in *Phantom* in one way or another.

Swan sits in the centre of a huge disc-shaped desk, designed to look like a giant gold record. His pose, arms outstretched, pre-empts Pacino's identical pose in his circular bath in *Scarface*.

The idea of having a video of oneself which ages and corrupts so that one's flesh doesn't is, of course, an updating of Oscar Wilde's *The Picture Of Dorian Gray*.

The split-screen sequence where The Phantom plants a bomb in The Beach Bums' stage car – is a homage to the celebrated opening 3-minute tracking shot of Welles' *Touch of Evil* (1958). Both sequences begin with a close-up of the bomb, and finish with a car exploding.

The motif of using disguised wipes during the long tracking shot – which De Palma took to ridiculous lengths in the opening reel of *Snake Eyes* – is a homage to Hitchcock's *Rope* (1948), which was made up of eight 10-minute takes (this was the greatest length of film a camera could then hold) which were joined together with cunningly hidden edits. Contrary to popular belief, there is actually one edit in *Rope* which isn't hidden – see if you can spot it. The sequence where The Phantom attacks Beef with a sink plunger is a very deliberate re-enactment of the shower scene from *Psycho*, now played for laughs as it has been innumerable times since. Later, Winslow watches the assassin take up his position in the auditorium, like Edna Best and Doris Day did in Hitchcock's 2 versions of *The Man Who Knew Too Much*.

De Palma paid tribute to his acting tutor and first producer - Wilford Leach, by *almost* naming The Phantom after him.

Artometer: 5/5

Obsession (1976)

The Cast: Cliff Robertson (Michael Courtland), Geneviève Bujold (Elizabeth Courtland/Sandra Portinari), John Lithgow[1] (Bob Lasalle), Wanda Blackman (Amy Courtland), Stanley J Reyes (Inspector Brie)

The Crew: Director: Brian De Palma, Writers: Brian De Palma & Paul Schrader, Producer: George Litto,[1] Composer: Bernard Herrmann,[2] Cinematographer: Vilmos Zsigmond,[1] Editor: Paul Hirsch[4]

Working Titles: Deja Vu, Double Ransom

The Plot: When Michael Courtland believes his wife Elizabeth and their daughter, Amy are kidnapped and accidentally killed, his life is over. He wanders through the next 16 years on autopilot, going through the motions of running a successful business, but garnering no pleasure from it. Then he meets his wife's spitting image, and he is drawn inescapably into a web of betrayal and deceit.

The Thickening: In this writer's opinion, this is De Palma's first minor work, because it follows the path of Hitchcock's *Vertigo* so slavishly, and Cliff Robertson's performance is a tribute to the finest polished mahogany. Nevertheless, the film's rather tasteless reversal of the Oedipal myth is dealt with subtlety, and there are some very complex, typically De Palmanian ideas just beneath the irritatingly soft-focus surface.

The Motifs. Colours: At the Courtland's party we close in on a waiter. Beneath his white coat, a gun is concealed. This threat beneath the surface is what the colour white is all about in a De Palma film. Little Amy's bedroom is all white frills and ruffles, so you know nothing good is going to happen there. It is worth noting that Bob dresses forever in summery white suits yet Michael, as befitting his life of mourning, opts more for funereal black. When Michael becomes more self-confident and begins to enact his obsessive fantasy, his demeanour changes and so does his wardrobe. The nastier he becomes, the lighter his suits are!

Doubles: Upon returning to Florence, Michael is drawn once again to the Church of San Miniato, where he first met Elizabeth, and here he happens to meet her spitting image. Because he desperately wants to believe what he sees, he doesn't pause to question this coincidence. After all, this is in a church, maybe miracles *do* happen!

The painting she is restoring is a Madonna by Bernardo Dadi (Daddy, geddit? All the hints are there!) The Madonna happens to have another, cruder painting beneath it, and the area to which Sandra is ministering, has two faces. So, in this tableau, we have the mother concealing another face and (did we but know it at this stage in the story) the daughter and the father. A fragmented family brought back together, after a fashion, beneath the arches of mother church. There is also the notion of virgin birth, and the possibility that a person's surface appearance may conceal a different interior. In essence the whole movie is cunningly summed up, right here.

Masks/Multiple Personas: The businessmen in the club all have gorgeous girls on their arms, yet unashamedly display portraits of their wives. They see nothing wrong in this infidelity – those damn continentals!

It comes as no great surprise at the dénouement when Bob announces that he has essentially been leading a double life – keeping Michael sweet all these years, whilst actually dealing against him in the cruellest manner imaginable.

Sandra also has two sides to her personality – there is the small child Amy, who was taken from her family in the most traumatic circumstances, and was then sold to her wicked 'uncle.' Then there is the girl who grew up believing she was a fatherless child called Sandra.

The Techniques. POV: When Amy is cut free from her mother, this is seen from her point of view. This is key in confusing the audience as to quite what is happening because this is the turning point in the film's narrative – did the unwary viewer but know it. Later, when the knowledge can be of no benefit, we see this sequence again, and this time we see the kidnapees being separated. Later, in a manner we will see De Palma use again and again, a journalist addresses the camera directly - providing exposition in as speedy a way as possible. Finally, when Sandra begins to remember her Amy self, she sees again everything she saw then – from the appropriate childish height. Bob's betrayal needs no explanation because we get to see it enacted in flashback.

Slow/Fast-Mo: Just to torture himself a little more, Michael allows himself to be drawn back to Florence, and then to San Miniato. He passes through its echoing interior in reflective slow motion. Because De Palma won't let the suspense drop until he absolutely has to, the film culminates with the maddened Michael and the suicidal Amy, running toward each other in slow motion – to attack each other or to greet each other? You just have to wait the long, torturous moments as they get closer to each other, to find out ...

Stories Within Stories: The film begins with a slide show, in memoriam of the church in Italy where Michael and his beloved Elizabeth first met. The image of this church needs to be planted in the audience's mind early on because it forms the model for the memorial he builds, and then becomes the location for his meeting with the second Elizabeth.

The truth of the kidnap drama, the death of her mother and Amy's subsequent sale to 'uncle' Bob, are all played out in flashback. The full-grown Sandra assumes the role of her childish Amy self, by simply having the camera looking down on her, as an adult looks down on a child.

Split-Screen: De Palma continues to explore the possibilities of the split-dioptre lens as an alternative to splitting the screen or editing back and forth. When Michael discusses money with Bob, he is in sharp focus in the foreground while Bob is in sharp focus in the background. This just emphasises the distance that now exists between their respective ambitions. In fact, if you see this film in its intended wide-screen ratio, you'll notice that Bob and Michael are frequently shown on opposite sides of the wide-screen frame.

41

Long Takes/Tracking Shots: One of De Palma's favourite moments in *Vertigo* is the spinning couple, with the camera turning one way and the couple turning the other to accentuate their rotation. He uses it here in an extended take of Michael and Elizabeth dancing, and introduces their beloved daughter. This moment is intentionally idyllic, so it contrasts with the nightmare of the kidnap. A similar rotation (achieved with a combination of camera movement and a dissolve) lasts some 16 years as Michael the younger builds a memorial to his lost love then transforms into Michael the elder, a man still haunted by his past, who has left millions of dollars worth of valuable land as an undeveloped park to Elizabeth and Amy's memory. How's that for a motive. Finally, Michael is reunited with his daughter in a long, rotating shot which evokes their last moment of pure happiness – the spinning dance, some 16 years earlier.

References: One hardly needs to mention that the idea of a heartbroken man finding the vision of his lost love, pursuing her, wooing her, transforming her and then finally being betrayed by her, is lifted wholly and unashamedly from Hitchcock's *Vertigo* (1958). The image of a car plunging into water will resurface again and again throughout De Palma's work. Opinion is divided as to the genesis of this interest – is it Teddy Kennedy's Chappaquiddick crash (considerably more on which can be found in *Blow Out*) or Norman Bates' penchant for sinking his victims in their cars into his local swamp in *Psycho* (1960). Here, it provides a conveniently messy end to Elizabeth and, supposedly, to Amy. Michael has left Amy's bedroom untouched, as a mouldering mausoleum to her. Much as Norman left his mother's bedroom untouched in *Psycho*. The climactic fight between Michael and Bob takes place over his desk and Bob is ultimately killed by a wickedly sharp pair of scissors – in a manner not greatly dissimilar to Grace Kelly's killing of Captain Lesgate in *Dial M For Murder* (1954).

Artometer: 4/5

Carrie (1976)

The Cast: Sissy Spacek (Carrie White), Piper Laurie (Margaret White), Amy Irving[1] (Sue Snell), William Katt (Tommy Ross), Nancy Allen[1] (Chris Hargenson), John Travolta[1] (Billy Nolan), Betty Buckley (Miss Collins), Cameron De Palma (Boy on Bicycle)

The Crew: Director: Brian De Palma, Writer: Lawrence D Cohen, Novel: Stephen King, Associate Producer: Louis A Stroller,[2] Composer:

Pino Donaggio,[1] Cinematographers: Mario Tosi (& Isidore Mankofsky, uncredited), Editor: Paul Hirsch[5]

The Plot: Carrie White develops telekinetic powers with the onset of adolescence. All the children at school torture her – so she kills them. Back home, Carrie's fanatically religious mother attacks her, so she kills her as well. And that's about it. We're not talking *War And Peace* here.

The Thickening: Building on the concerns he had dealt with in *Obsession*, De Palma makes *Carrie* into another film knee-deep in religious imagery. Religious intolerance is very often present as a sub-plot in Stephen King's works, but most film adaptations ignore it. De Palma increases it!

The Themes. Sexism: The misogyny demonstrated here stems from Carrie's mother, who reads from *The Sin Of Women* and blames Carrie for 'the curse of blood.' Clearly she is insane and is unable to deal with the self-imposed guilt over having ever fallen pregnant herself. Strangely, one feels that this sub-plot must have had some autobiographical resonance for De Palma, whose mother unashamedly admits he was an unwanted 'mistake.' One can imagine that he must have spent a lot of time as a child wishing he could just make everyone go away by a simple act of will.

The Motifs. Colours: The shower room is filled with steam which is filled with clean white light. This is then stained with red as Carrie begins to bleed. And so she begins and ends the film, stained with blood. Carrie and Margaret White both have red hair. In this context, red is very much the colour of power, it accompanies the birth of the power (the menstrual blood) and then it instigates the uncontrolled use of those powers (the pigs' blood). Conversely, red is also the catalyst which makes that power so violent: Tommy and Billy both drive red cars. The bucket of pigs' blood is obtained by Billy in a red shirt wielding a red hammer. Finally, when Carrie, dowsed in red blood, unleashes a lifetime's pent-up fury - the lights at the Prom all turn red.

White, the usual colour of evil in a De Palma movie, is also present: for example, in Carrie's surname, which she has inherited from her malevolent mother. The sun-bleached walls of the school, where so much cruelty is acted out, are white. The interfering gym teacher's blood spattered shorts and socks are also white. The significance of white and red is made apparent by Carrie's Prom dress, which is pink – red and white mixed.

After all hell literally breaks loose at the school, Carrie goes home – her dress, hair and skin now dyed livid red. A bright red fire engine roars past, followed by Travolta's bright red car, which bursts into flames with a glance from Carrie. When she leaves the gym it is a blackened husk, burning orange at the windows and doorways. This is the medieval hell Carrie has left in her wake. When she arrives home, it too is lit with hellish orange. The gym was filled with uncontrollable flame. Home is stacked high with candles. Mother has created a little domestic version of hell.

Doubles: When Miss Collins is attempting to make Carrie feel good about herself, they are both reflected in a mirror. This suggests a bond of identification between them, implying that Miss Collins must have suffered her share of bullying at school and can't now bear to see it going unpunished.

The Techniques. POV: When Sue sees the rope running up the side of the stage to the rafters above, we follow her line of sight. We finally figure out what Billy and Chris were up to the night before, and what their big plan was, as Sue likewise figures it out.

Slow/Fast-Mo: The communal shower scene is shot in dreamy slow motion, to accentuate the pleasure Carrie feels just spending a moment by herself, being ignored by the girls who hate her. When Carrie wins at the Prom, she is bathed in white light and, to the accompaniment of the same romantic theme, walks up to collect her prize. Once again, she is totally immersed in enjoying herself, and gets to savour every last moment. While she can.

The bucket falling and spraying Carrie is in traditional De Palmanian slow-mo. The conversion to slow motion in a De Palma film is generally accompanied by the sound being reduced to the bare minimum to focus the viewer's mind on what is important. Here we get the bucket clanking and the sound of liquid dripping, but no dialogue.

Stories Within Stories: With the mother no longer there to restrain her, Carrie's power is unleashed and she, her mother and their entire house is drawn down into hell. After this, Sue, the lone survivor, dreams of taking flowers to mark Carrie's passing and, in a purely visceral moment, which serves no purpose but to send teenage cinema audiences out into the street buzzing with excitement, she is grabbed by Carrie's arm from beneath the ground.

Split-Screen: Although this film features De Palma's most widely-known use of split-screen – and the one that other film-makers inevitably quote when they are justifying their own use of it – I personally don't feel it adds anything to the Prom sequence. Better use might well have been made if we had seen the bucket before spillage on one side of the screen, and Carrie's joy on the other – then leave the action to carry its own momentum. This would seem to be more in-keeping with De Palma's usual habit of using the split to compare parallel and simultaneous events which add tension to each other.

Long Takes/Tracking Shots: Once we arrive at the Prom, we are treated to a long overhead boom shot, taking in the whole crowd. Then we get Tommy and Carrie's lengthy rotating dance and finally the evidence of the ballot being rigged, followed by a swoop up into the roof to get a good look at the bucket of blood, then across to Tommy and Carrie winning the Prom Couple contest.

References: The slow-mo shower scene at the beginning is the same opening image which De Palma uses 4 years later in *Dressed To Kill*. When Carrie is sitting outside the Principle's office, we can see over her shoulder into the office. De Palma re-used this over-the-shoulder framework in *Dressed To Kill* and *Raising Cain*. Carrie's use of her powers, is always accompanied by the stab of Herrmannesque *Psycho* strings. In an alteration from the source novel, De Palma elects to call the school Bates High. The rotating dance at the Prom is De Palma reusing the *Vertigo*-inspired moment he last used in *Obsession*.

Margaret White's impaling with kitchen knives, whilst echoing the statue of St Sebastian she keeps in her closet, is also an allusion to Toshiro Mifune's death by a hail of arrows in *Throne Of Blood* (1957), Kurosawa's allegorical rendition of Macbeth.

Artometer: 3/5

The Fury (1978)

The Cast: Kirk Douglas[1] (Peter Sandza), John Cassavetes (Childress), Amy Irving[2] (Gillian Bellaver), Carrie Snodgress (Hester), Charles Durning[3] (Dr McKeever), Andrew Stevens (Robin Sandza), Fiona Lewis (Dr Susan Charles), William Finley[6] (Raymond Dunwoodie), Dennis Franz[1] (Bob The Cop), Daryl Hannah (Pam)

The Crew: Director: Brian De Palma. Writer/Novel: John Farris, Producers: Jack B Bernstein & Ron Preissman & Frank Yablans, Composer: John Williams, Cinematographer: Richard H Kline, Editor: Paul Hirsch[6]

The Plot: Peter Sandza works for the secret service. His son, Robin develops telekinetic powers so Peter's employer, his best friend Childress, kidnaps his son and endeavours to kill Peter.

A year later, Peter is still deep under cover, attempting to rescue his son and kill Childress. Meanwhile, at The Paragon Institute, Gillian Bellaver is a young girl who is developing telekinetic powers. She crosses Peter's path and together they learn about the terrible things Childress has done to Robin.

The Thickening: De Palma cheerfully admits that he was re-making *Carrie* and this was simply another attempt by him to get his foot in the door of Hollywood. I suppose, if we are to be generous, we can look upon *The Fury* as a thematic sequel to *Carrie*, with Sissy Spacek having transferred her powers to Amy Irving. Personally I suspect De Palma was more drawn to the cloak-and-dagger aspect of the plot. He did not do a proper espionage movie until *Mission:Impossible*.

In much the way that De Palma presumably saw something of his own childhood in the relationship between Carrie and Margaret, so it is possible that this film, being about distant fathers, may also carry personal resonance for him. Childress tells Gillian, "I'll be a good father to you Gillian. You can rely on that." It is not a coincidence that his name is but one letter away from 'childless.' Much of the film turns on the desire to be a good, protective father.

The Themes. Sexism: Simply being a doctor, doesn't preclude Dr Charles from being a sex worker. She is Robin's ball and chain, keeping him passive with casual, uncomplicated sex. Unfortunately, she makes herself too easy to have, and so Robin begins to treat her at first with contempt and eventually with extreme violence. From here onwards, women who are either promiscuous for the fun of it, or are paid sex workers, became a constant feature of De Palma films.

Violence: Whenever Gillian uses her power, she causes bleeding. This serves to put the viewer in mind of the relationship between blood and telepathy De Palma established in *Carrie*. Also, when Gillian grips McKeever's hand and feels all the pain of the wound he has there – one is put in mind of stigmatic wounds. Where McKeever has a wounded hand, Childress has a deadened arm. When Gillian lets her energy out, her victim, Ellen, pours blood from her eyes, ears, mouths and, probably most disturbingly, from beneath her fingernails. This confirms the connection between psychokinetics and blood, and continues to tie this all in with notions of stigmatisation.

Hester dies messily, (as increasingly becomes the case in De Palma's films) smashed through a car windscreen and left bleeding on its hood. Gillian, like Robin before her, has had all childish innocence beaten out of her. First. she blinds Childress with a kiss, drawing gouts of blood out of his eyes, then kills him in the most explosive way seen on screen at that time. So shocking, in fact, is Childress' death, that De Palma treats us to it no fewer than 13 times. Finishing with a view from on high, looking down, Godlike, at the carnage below.

Voyeurism/Surveillance: While Peter is under attack from Childress' men, he is being filmed. Although it is not quite clear why, at least retrieving the film serves to mark Childress out as the bad guy. We are introduced to Gillian while the esper-hunter, Dunwoodie, is following her. Since she is wearing her bikini, the first thought is that this sweaty, greasy man is following her for reasons other than to report her telepathic abilities to Peter. As it happens, he is being bugged, recorded and filmed himself. They don't leave anything to chance these Secret Service types. They post agents all over the street Peter was last seen on, just waiting for him to re-emerge. When he does, disguised as an old man, Childress doesn't need to be psychic to see straight through the disguise, because he knows Peter's methods.

When Gillian is investigating Robin's room, her power turns her into a human surveillance instrument, eavesdropping on conversations Robin had had in that room months previously.

The Motifs. Colours: The showdown between Robin and his 'lover' Dr Barnes takes place in a chilly white room. Uh-oh, duck. No, it's too late. Robin's arrogance boils over into psychosis when he telekinetically lifts Barnes up and spins her madly in the air. Her blood sprays the snowy white walls.

Doubles: Gillian's powers begin to resemble Robin's. "You're like twins!" Now she has sensed his pain, she can tell how he is. She becomes Peter's connection to his son. When Childress is attempting to lie to Gillian, he is reflected in a mirrored wall, implying his double-dealing, two-faced nature.

Masks/Multiple Personas: Being spies, Childress and Peter are practised in enacting alternative roles. For example, Childress has been pretending to be Peter's friend for long enough for the fiction to take. After escaping their clutches, in only his y-fronts, Peter has to make a quick stop to change. Some borrowed clothing, a little padding, polish in his hair to make him grey, and off he goes, a frail old man. The Institute Gillian goes to, is actually an undercover recruitment centre of telepathic children for the secret services.

The Techniques. POV: In her second flashback, Gillian sees from Robin's perspective as he is strapped to various machines which monitor his responses. When Robin is dying, he passes his immense power to Gillian through his eyes. They are the windows to the soul, you know!

Slow/Fast-Mo: Hester and Gillian's escape from The Institute is presented as an extended slow motion sequence with, as we have come to expect from De Palma, very carefully selected sound effects punctuating the silence. Here we have gunshots and car crashes and Williams' soaring music, but no dialogue. This was, for many years, my favourite De Palma sequence, possibly because it succeeds so perfectly in making the obscene poetic.

Stories Within Stories: When Peter is under attack on the beach, we see much of his activities in a frame-in-frame from the point of view of the camera recording his exploits.

Gillian gets flash-forwards of traumatic events from her future. The first of these is a sudden shocking view of the mutilated Dr Charles from the very end of the movie. This is the first time De Palma teased us by showing us the film's end before we've even got a handle on its beginning. He used very different techniques to achieve a similar end in *Carlito's Way* and *Mission:Impossible*.

Curiously, she also gets flashbacks, when they are dramatically convenient, such as the flashback of Robin she gets from touching McKeever's hand. During the second of these, when she is experiencing Robin's pain directly, we finally learn why his father's supposed assassination was filmed, so they could show him the footage and measure his emotional reactions to it!

Split-Screen: When Gillian first demonstrates her power, it is on a model train in focus in the extreme foreground, while her reaction is in focus in the background. This is the only time I can recall a horizontal split-dioptre lens being used.

Long Takes/Tracking Shots: Gillian's integration into the Paragon Institute is seen through an extended shot of her playing computer games, with jump-cuts removing all the boring bits. Later, when she is getting to know Hester as they eat breakfast, the camera slowly dollies in a semicircle around them, just as it had on the beach when Robin and his father had been discussing their future at a beach-side table.

References: John Williams' score is a very obvious and, one can assume, deliberate homage to Herrmann. This is ironic since Williams was producer Litto's first choice to score *Obsession*, until editor Paul Hirsch and De Palma persuaded him to approach Herrmann. The school environment, and the distress caused by Gillian's emerging powers, make the film's early scenes seem very similar to *Carrie*. De Palma's desire to cast John Cassavetes was helped by his enthusiasm for Cassavetes' performance as the manipulative, immoral Guy Woodhouse in Polanski's

Rosemary's Baby (1968), a film which De Palma said had a direct influence on *Sisters*. Peter Sandza's roof-top struggle with his son is framed and edited in much the way Hitchcock shot the rooftop climax of *To Catch A Thief* (1955).

Artometer: 2/5

Home Movies (1979)

The Cast: Keith Gordon[1] (Denis Byrd), Gerrit Graham[4] (James Byrd), Nancy Allen[2] (Kristina), Vincent Gardenia (Dr Byrd), Mary Davenport[2] (Mrs Byrd), Kirk Douglas[2] (The Maestro)

The Crew: Director: Brian De Palma, Writers: Kim Ambler & Dana Edelman & Robert Harders & Stephen Lemay & Gloria Norris, Producer: Sam Irvin, Composer: Pino Donaggio,[2] Cinematographer: James L Carter, Editor: Corky O'Hara

The Plot: Denis Byrd is one very confused teenager. His father is a doctor whose philandering has driven his mother into depression and fake suicide attempts. The light of her life is her eldest son, James, who is a teacher at the nearby college. who leads his students in a physical exercise program he calls 'Spartanetics' which is really just a sublimation of his homosexuality. Feeling even more alone in the world than most teenagers do, Denis becomes fixated on James' ex-prostitute girlfriend, Kristina and determines to save her from James' cruel manipulations. Meanwhile, enter The Maestro, a college professor who tries a little 'Star Therapy' on Denis, ordering him to keep a filmed diary, thus making himself the star of his life's movie. Denis decides to use his new camera to film his father's infidelity, to help his mother get a divorce and thereby become the 'hero' of his own life.

The Thickening: It is ironic that this most personal of De Palma's projects, should also be his most collaborative. Having returned to his alma mater, Sarah Lawrence College, to teach Film Studies, he chose to do so by giving his students first-hand experience of actually making a movie – with a big Hollywood star thrown in for good measure!

The painfully autobiographical elements in the film relate to Denis' family's resemblance to De Palma's own: a distant and unfaithful father who was a doctor; a depressive mother who doted on her eldest son; an intelligent if overly ambitious younger son, desperate to earn his mother's approval. De Palma freely admits that, at the age of 16, he put his father under surveillance in an attempt to catch him out in his infidelities. This sort of story would, he must have realised, make a great movie. And so he turned his own dysfunctional childhood into *Home Movies*.

Given that there was an entire class full of cooks stirring this broth (under De Palma's direction, admittedly) it was inevitable that *Home Movies* is a somewhat uneven film. There were, for example, no fewer than 6 writers contributing to the screenplay, each bringing their own agendas and voices. Some of the comedy - particularly scenes involving James' domination of Kristina - are more interesting thematically than they are funny.

Arguably, the most valuable lesson De Palma taught his students – was about their likely treatment at the hands of studios. Because he wanted *Home Movies* to be a real, professional movie from beginning to end, he set about trying to find distribution for it. In the end, United Artists optioned it, but paid no money up front, promising, instead, a high percentage of the profit. But they didn't market the film properly, so it died at the box office, and profits are hard to make under such circumstances.

Finally, a note must be made of the fact that this entire endeavour could take place purely because De Palma, his good friends Steven Spielberg and George Lucas, and the film's star, Kirk Douglas, contributed the lion's share of the film's $400,000 budget, just to ensure that this unique experiment in on-the-job training could go ahead.

Artometer: 4/5

(Note: Because this film was never released in Britain, and remains unavailable on video anywhere; I have derived almost all the above information from the writings of Bill Fentum. Feel free to check out his website 'briandepalma.net' for far more detail on *Home Movies*. No, that's all right, off you go. I'll wait.)

The Eighties: When You Get The Money, You Get The Power!

Dressed To Kill (1980)

The Cast: Michael Caine (Dr Robert Elliott), Angie Dickinson (Kate Miller), Nancy Allen[3] (Liz Blake), Keith Gordon[2] (Peter Miller), Dennis Franz[2] (Detective Marino), David Margulies (Dr Levy), Susanna Clemm (Betty Luce/'Bobbi'), William Finley[7] (Bobbi's Phone Voice), Mary Davenport[3] (Shocked Woman in Restaurant)

The Crew: Writer/Director: Brian De Palma, Producers: Samuel Z Arkoff & Fred C Caruso[1] & George Litto,[2] Composer: Pino Donaggio,[3] Cinematographer: Ralf D Bode, Editor: Gerald B Greenberg[1]

The Plot: Kate Miller is an unsatisfied wife. She plays a potentially dangerous game with a man she meets in an art gallery. He takes her home. They have sex. While her lover sleeps, she leaves and is brutally murdered by a strange woman in an elevator. Prostitute Liz Blake witnessed the assault, so she and Kate's teenage son Peter set about figuring out who the strange woman is, and what connection she has with Kate's psychiatrist Dr Elliott.

The Thickening: With the debatable exception of *Scarface*, this is De Palma's most controversial film. Feminist theorists could no longer ignore him after the out and out assault they saw this film-making on women – and he became the resident bad guy on Film Studies courses from then onwards. I suppose it's a form of notoriety.

This film was subjected to greater censorship in the UK than any of his previous films although, predictably, it was Angie Dickinson's opening masturbation scene which was most severely cut, not the brutal attack on her. There is a well-established argument that, at least as far as British censorship goes, sex is considered so unhealthy it has to be removed, whilst murderous violence must be okay because it is toned down, but rarely cut out.

The Themes. Sexism: Okay, fair enough. The representation of a woman who is sexually frustrated so picks up the first likely candidate she meets and goes back to his place for a dose of unprotected humpage, doesn't say much for liberated women of the fledgling eighties. Similarly, having her hacked to death as punishment, seems overly-judgmental. Then, to add insult to injury, the woman who helps solve the puzzle is another of De Palma's sex workers.

Since Nancy Allen was De Palma's wife at the time, one has to wonder why he felt the need to degrade her as he does in this film and *Blow Out*. Similarly, in *Bonfire*, he spent a day filming his then girlfriend, Beth Broderick squirming with discomfort and embarrassment with her knickers in her hand and her arse on a photocopier. It is almost as if he wants to punish those who love him. Or am I starting to sound like a mad psychiatrist?

Violence: As is now often the case with De Palma, when Kate dies, she dies messily and slowly – repeatedly hacked with a straight-razor.

Voyeurism/Surveillance: In the art gallery, Kate finds herself eavesdropping on other people's conversations. Peeping into their private lives, and taking a cheap vicarious thrill from the experience. In the police station, Peter bugs the detective's office, so he can hear the psychiatrist's testimony. Later, he sets up an ingenious camera to film all the patients coming in and out of Elliott's office. In much the way The Phantom once stood in the pouring rain to watch his beloved through a window, and Carlito will also, Peter stands out in a downpour and watches as Liz undresses in Elliott's apartment.

The Motifs. Colours: In the art gallery, Kate is dressed all in white. The man on whom she fixes her gaze, is similarly monochromatic – being dressed in black. Since white is generally the colour of malice and guilt in a De Palma film, this implies, at least to me, that De Palma is exonerating the black-clad man from culpability in what is about to happen to Kate. In Liz's dream of the asylum – a place bathed in overpowering blue – 'Bobbi' attacks her nurse, rather like Carrie attacking Sue in her dream at the end of *Carrie*.

Doubles: When Kate asks Elliott why he doesn't sleep with her, he looks at himself in the mirror – at the other side of himself, his double – to be reminded of why he doesn't. Whenever Elliott realises he is aroused, he has to look at himself in a mirror, to see if he's still himself – checking his sexual identity. The film ends as it begins, with a woman, naked and vulnerable in the shower, being attacked. In both cases it is a fantasy. But some fantasies are more positive than others.

Masks/Multiple Personas: Of course, what has put everyone off the scent is that the evidence shows a 'woman' as the likely perpetrator. No one stops to think that it might be someone in disguise. When Elliott goes to see 'Bobbi's' psychiatrist – they discuss 'her' on the stairs. Several key moments in De Palma films occur on stairs – the showdown in *Scarface*, the confrontation between Ness and Capone, then the climactic shoot-out, in *The Untouchables*, and the revelation of the defence contract conspiracy in *Snake Eyes*, to name the most obvious. Stairs are transitional places, where things change. In *Dressed To Kill*, this staircase scene is the one which confirms Elliott's involvement in Kate's death, although we still don't know to what extent.

The Techniques. POV: The main use of POV here comes from the perspective of the maniac during his pursuit of his victim. This keeps 'Bobbi' out of the shot, which conveniently allows De Palma to avoid giving 'her' a close-up and thereby giving the game away.

Slow/Fast-Mo: As with *Carrie*, the opening shower sequence is shot in languorous slow-mo, to emphasis the pleasure and relaxation of the woman in question. When Liz witnesses Kate's murder, the moment is drawn out to emphasise its shocking brutality. When Peter is investigating the doctor, he watches his madly speeded-up film of all of Elliott's patients coming and going.

Stories Within Stories: Elliott sits in his office and watches *Donahue* on television, interviewing transsexuals – implanting the notion in the viewer's mind for later reference. De Palma cuts back and forth between Elliott and Liz watching the same programme, thereby uniting the hunter with his eventual prey.

Split-Screen: As Kate begins to feel guilty about what she's done, she has flashbacks to things she has discarded in her passion – her gloves and her wedding ring. These flashbacks are presented as split-screen images.

The film's most celebrated use of split-screen, also serves to mislead the audience in the most cunning manner, by seemingly having both 'Bobbi' and Elliott on camera at the same time when, in fact, 'Bobbi' is Betty Luce, an undercover police officer.

The split-dioptre shot is used for comedy when Liz and Peter are discussing, in explicit detail, a sex-change operation, whilst a rather prissy looking woman behind them, who is eavesdropping, slowly goes white with shock.

Long Takes/Tracking Shots: For almost 9 minutes, Kate pursues her man around the art-gallery in an elaborate sequence of fluid tracking shots, all stitched together without a word of significant dialogue. In fact, there is almost no dialogue for the remaining 10 minutes of the film in which she is alive. This lays the groundwork for extended virtually-silent sequences in *Body Double* and *Mission:Impossible*.

References: The opening scene of Kate masturbating in the shower, then fantasising about being raped in there, draws on the opening scene of *Carrie* as well as the notorious shower scene in *Psycho*. De Palma will again play with this image in the opening film-in-film of *Blow Out*, and the closing film-in-film of *Body Double*. Personally, I think he just likes filming women in showers!

Killing the female lead about 30 minutes in has parallels to *Psycho*, as well as *Sisters*.

Young Peter's engineering precocity and his fanatical surveillance of his suspect, mirrors De Palma's own childhood. This is the third film in succession which has had obvious parallels with De Palma's childhood. Clearly the man who demonstrates little or no public emotion, suffers deep emotion wounds which he has to attempt to heal through thinly-veiled confession. Much like the rest of us.

Unlike *Sisters*, here De Palma elects to employ the *Psycho* method and simply have a psychiatrist explain the Elliott/Bobbi duality.

Before getting his big break in Hollywood, De Palma wrote an adaptation of Gerald Walker's novel *Cruising*, about a series of murders in New York. This included a sequence where a woman named Kate picks up a man at a museum, spends the afternoon with him and, finding that he has VD, leaves in a flurry only to be stabbed to death in the elevator by the lurking murderer. *Cruising* (1980) went on to be directed by William Friedkin, but without this sequence. So, waste not want not, De Palma used it!

Artometer: 3/5

Blow Out (1981)

The Cast: John Travolta[2] (Jack), Nancy Allen[4] (Sally), John Lithgow[2] (Burke), Dennis Franz[3] (Manny Karp), Curt May (Frank Donahue)

The Crew: Writer/Director: Brian De Palma, Producers: Fred C Caruso[2] & George Litto,[3] Composer: Pino Donaggio,[4] Cinematographer: Vilmos Zsigmond,[2] Editor: Paul Hirsch[7]

Working Title: Personal Effects

The Plot: Jack is an unwitting witness to an assassination, but only realises this when he plays back his audio recording of the events and hears the gunshot. Burke, the renegade (and somewhat incompetent) assassin, has created a terrible mess by killing politician MacRyan in front of no fewer than three witnesses, two of whom recorded the event – so he decides to tie up all the loose ends in a particularly nasty way.

The Thickening: Building on the nerd-as-hero motif of *Dressed To Kill*, this film similarly features a protagonist who started out as the kid who won the science-fairs, just as De Palma himself did, and eventually became practised in surveillance techniques.

Governor MacRyan, in the car, is utterly irrelevant to the story. His only purpose is to give the characters something to tussle over – a shame De Palma didn't go the whole hog and call this character Governor MacGuffin.

The Themes. Violence: Burke's predilection for garrotting women makes for some deeply disturbing visuals, consciously designed, I feel, to remind the viewer of *Dressed To Kill*. After all the controversy surrounding the violence to women in that film, it seems De Palma wanted the world to know that he was unrepentant.

Voyeurism/Surveillance: When he is out recording wildtrack sound, Jack catches a snatch of a conversation, so turns and listens to the lovers. In the hospital, he tells Sally she must stay under observation and she states, simply but emphatically "I don't want to be observed." It will soon come to light that she actually makes a living by being observed and indeed photographed – by Karp – in bed with the rich and gullible. The only background we get on Jack – apart from the revelation that he was (and is) the kind of kid who takes electrical objects to pieces – is that he worked as a surveillance expert for the police, and an officer was killed whilst under his supervision. When Jack is hiding the precious film behind his ceiling panels, we watch through his window – heightening the feeling of paranoia which pervades the film. Later, Jack's telephone conversation with the reporter, Donahue, is see through the window, so we can follow the wires to Burke's tap and observe him eavesdropping on their plans.

The Motifs. Colours: The entrance to the hospital where Jack takes Sally is red – the hospital beyond is white. It is here that the conspiracy to cover up the assassination is hatched.

When Jack persuades Sally to stay and help him sort out the crime, they are bathed in empowering red light.

When Sally goes to visit Karp in his hideout, it has grimy red walls and is lit by the livid red neon sign outside the window. So, we know he's safe, he lives in the red. Jack, on the other hand, lives in a house with white walls... ooh.

The old red, white and blue features throughout this tale of political double-dealing: in the motel wallpaper, Jack and Sally's blue and red shirts as they argue over their next move, the political badge Burke wears in the final scenes, even 2 cement trucks Sally passes on her first visit to Karp's apartment. On Liberty Day, in front of a huge stars and stripes flag, Jack, Sally and Burke are bathed in the light of alternating red, white and blue fireworks. As Jack cradles Sally, lit only by the light of these explosions, the black night gives way to the white of the next day's snow and Jack is found sitting alone in the park, buried deep in his own guilt.

Doubles: Burke attempts to follow Sally with the intention of murdering her. Unfortunately, his reflexes are not what they could be and the woman he ends up murdering isn't Sally. However, she did look like her from the back. Later, he claims this murder was to create the notion of a serial killer, to cover up his intended assassination of Sally. Whether this is true, or if he is, in fact, killing purely for pleasure, is never fully explored.

His second victim, the hooker in the station toilet, is another dead ringer for Sally, but this time he knows it isn't really her. This attack would seem to be purely by way of a warming up exercise and a way of continuing his established pattern of Liberty Bell Stranglings.

The Techniques. POV: This film begins with a protracted POV sequence – the traditional stalker in the bushes type of thing, culminating in the inevitable attack in the shower, all of which turns out to be a film within the film. Sally's double is pursued through a crowded market – seen entirely from her pursuer's perspective.

Slow/Fast-Mo: The primary example of slow motion here is when Jack is panicking and running to rescue Sally. To extend the tension of this moment, De Palma slows Jack down to a crawl for the duration of his flight through the crowd and up the stairs. Even so, you know he'll get there just in the nick of time... don't you?

Stories Within Stories: The opening POV sequence is, in fact, from the horror film Jack is working on. Governor MacRyan is introduced through Jack's television, which tells all about his election campaign and popularity. When Jack gets hold of Karp's photographs, he assembles them into an improbably smooth animation of the car crash. When played out with his recording, this tells its own tale about the crash.

When Sally's story comes to an end, with a terrified scream, he will splice this into his film as punishment of himself. A momento mori. This is not a film about triumph. Unlike most fictions, clean solutions don't rise conveniently out of the murky waters of political expediency. So Jack is left alone, crushed by a conspiracy he never came close to understanding. All he knows is that someone else under his care has died.

Split-Screen: Whilst Jack is absent-mindedly listening to the television report on one side of the screen, he is splicing together all of his sound-effects and labelling them dispassionately: 'Body fall,' for example. This disassembles some of the magic of cinema – much as the split-screen technique can.

The first examples of extreme distance between the foreground and background, comes with Jack's night-time recording session, where we see him way over in the distance, and the frog and owl he is recording are in the extreme foreground.

Much later, Burke waits for Sally, armed with a photo of her, in the extreme foreground of a split-dioptre shot, whilst her unfortunate double walks past in the background.

Long Takes/Tracking Shots: The only long tracking shot is when Jack finds that one of his tapes has been wiped – he checks another, then another, then moves around the room, checking more and more tapes on different machines, all in one extended, rotating shot which, when the full calamity has been realised, cuts to an intimidating overhead shot.

References: It probably isn't a coincidence that the reporter is named Donahue – after Phil Donahue, the TV presenter featured in *Dressed To Kill*. The sequence where Jack assembles Karp's photos into a motion picture, complete with his sound, is an update of the forensic sequence from *Blow-Up*. Sharp readers may have noticed a certain titular similarity with this film as well. Intimately involved with this obsessive dissection of film and photos – is the legendary 'Zapruder Film' of the Kennedy assassination, which Karp insists his photos are the biggest thing since. The car careering into a lake with a mysterious girl in it, bears more than a cursory similarity to Teddy Kennedy's 1969 Chappaquiddick car crash which brought his presidential aspirations to an end. So, De Palma's long-standing obsession with the Kennedies and their integral involvement in the collapse of the sixties, was still fresh in his mind.

Artometer: 4/5

Scarface (1983)

The Cast: Al Pacino[1] (Tony Montana), Steven Bauer[1] (Manny), Michelle Pfeiffer (Elvira Hancock), Mary Elizabeth Mastrantonio (Gina Montana), Robert Loggia (Frank Lopez), F Murray Abraham[1] (Omar Suarez), Paul Shenar (Alejandro Sosa), Gregg Henry[1] (uncredited cameo)

The Crew: Director: Brian De Palma, Writer: Oliver Stone, Novel: Armitage Trail, Original Screenplay: Howard Hawks, Producers: Martin Bregman[1] & Peter Saphier & Louis A Stroller,[3] Composer: Giorgio Moroder, Cinematographer: John A Alonzo,[2] Editors: Gerald B Greenberg[2] & David Ray[1]

The Plot: Arriving in America as part of Castro's evacuation of Cuba's prisons, Tony Montana is already a hardened criminal. He sees the States as a chance for him to realise his ambition to have "what's coming to me... the world and everything in it." Soon he has negotiated his way into Frank Lopez's drug business. Progressively, his arrogance growing at a similar pace to his paranoia, he builds his own massive drugs empire, but betrays and executes so many of the people around him that he finds there is nothing left for him to do but defend himself.

The Thickening: After *Blow Out*, De Palma decided it was time for another change of direction. He had spent more than 10 years honing his visual grammar skills. It was time to put his Hitchcock phase behind him and move towards the Hollywood mainstream and the financial security that offered.

Then the explosive script for *Scarface* came along. Written by Oliver Stone, the film would need a director unafraid of controversy, as it would doubtless attract criticism for its depiction of race, organised crime, drug abuse and, most of all, violence. This wasn't the sort of script a Hollywood mainstreamer could really do justice to. But De Palma, who was already perceived as a Hollywood outsider, well, he had nothing to lose.

The Themes. Violence: One hardly need mention the violence in *Scarface*. The chainsaw in the bathroom sequence was probably the one scene which haunted the censorship debate throughout the eighties, only to be replaced after some 8 years by *Reservoir Dogs'* ear-cutting scene. In common with most moments of De Palmanian violence, it involves white walls being sprayed with a substantial amount of red blood.

Voyeurism/Surveillance: During Tony's show-wedding, we get the first glimpse of his paranoia. He has bought himself a palatial mansion, and surrounded it with surveillance cameras. The final days of Tony's life – his time as Nebuchadnezzar, conquering lord of all Babylon - begins with a close-up of his 6 security monitors, which he watches morbidly. He admits that he spends 12% of his profits on surveillance. Ironically, when the cameras warn him of the approach of Sosa's vengeful army, he is too wrapped-up in his own incestuous rage and self-pity to even glance at the monitors which have cost him so much.

The Motifs. Colours: Colour is more conspicuously important in *Scarface* than in any of De Palma's previous films – even *Sisters*. The original movie poster was a striking black and white image, cut down the middle so the background was pure black on one side, pure white on the other. De Palma hired Ferdinando Scarfiotti as visual consultant for this film and, I suspect, orchestrating its careful, thematic use of colour, would be one of his primary responsibilities.

Rebenga, Castro's old torturer who Tony has to kill to secure his freedom, is dressed all in white. The white-is-evil correlation will never be more clearly defined than in this film where, of course, the Bolivian marching powder which fuels all of the chaos, is pure white. *Miami Vice*, the definitive American television show of the eighties, also flooded the screen with bleached and designer whites, behind which untold corruption took place.

When Tony kills Rebenga, he is wearing a red T-shirt – the colour of blood and transition.

In this film, De Palma introduces the colour orange into his regular palette, especially in connection with sunsets. Miami is first seen as an idyllic sunset which is, in fact, painted on the side of a building. A similar painted sunset decorates the wall of the hotel room where the drugs buy goes so disastrously wrong. Later, when Tony makes his demand to meet Frank, and thereby force his way onto the ladder of success, he does so against the background of a real, vividly orange sunset.

Frank's palatial home, which is both evil (it is bought with drug money) and transitional (it gives Tony his first taste of immense wealth), has stark white walls with conspicuous red details – carpets, ornaments, etc. Frank wears a white suit. His office, by contrast, is black with red highlights – and a painted orange sunset running all down one wall.

The first time we see Tony snort coke is very possibly his first time he ever has, and it is given to him by Elvira, who is dressed all in white. Fuelled by the drug, he promptly attacks her.

By the time Tony has become a big man in his own right, and starts throwing money at his mother, he has a white suit of his own, worn with a contrasting black shirt. This is the colour of his power and corruption. Much later, when he is powerless and the corruption has taken him over completely, his clothing will be the reverse of this – a black suit with white shirt.

When Tony goes to Columbia and makes the deal which will set him up in his own business – he wears the empowering red shirt. The Babylon, the nightclub he comes to look upon as his own, has red doors. The bent cop (Bernstein) he meets there, wears the obligatory white suit. His first showdown with his promiscuous sister, is in one of the Babylon's toilets – all gleaming in white, with black marble fixtures. The black and white locale is particularly ironic, since his motives for keeping Manny and Gina away from each other are never less than grey.

Once Tony has acquired his money, power and woman, the colour-scheme of his life loses the white, and runs more towards the blacks and reds. More befitting a man-made hell! More indicative of the fact that his ambition has about run out. All that is left for him now is violence.

The gallery in which he hangs the portrait of himself and his wife, has very deliberate red walls. Implying that their marriage is all about power, not about love. The carpets and corridors around Tony's office are red, whilst the walls and his throne are jet black.

When Tony returns to Colombia, to Sosa's for a council of war, they meet in a room of red walls. So now we know from where the violence comes.

As his last ragged breath leaves him, Tony falls forward and explodes into a final gush of red blood, as he falls into his own fountain. The red aggression of his ambition brought him all the money and power he wanted, and the red of aggression finally collected the bill.

Doubles: As Tony begins to show the first signs of breaking under the strain of his own ambition, he sits in his mirrored booth, alone, his own head reflected back at himself from several different angles, illustrating that he is beginning to live in a world which requires him to develop new skills, and new personality traits. These heads are all turned away from him, possibly implying that he isn't capable of this much transformation. He will remain a barely-literate thug.

The Techniques. Slow/Fast-Mo: When Tony's career takes an upswing, time flies by in the form of a montage. We see hints of Tony's enormous wealth, and his spectacular wedding to Elvira. It is not without significance that we don't actually see them happy together. As so often happens with moments of extreme pain – De Palma extends the moment when Tony learns the truth about Manny and Gina, by reducing the sound to the bare minimum (the gunshots), and slowing the motion down. The next slow motion sequence also involves guns and stairs – as Tony engages in a ferocious shoot-out with his military-style heavy ordnance.

Split-Screen: In his office he has 6 security monitors, watching different sides of his house. In his huge bathroom, he has 5 television screens, offering him 5 simultaneous distractions from his own life.

Long Takes/Tracking Shots: When Tony is caught in a sting operation, laundering vast quantities of money, the scene continues as a protracted take, all under the watchful eye of the camera hidden in the clock. When his marriage is finally falling apart, along with any vestige of self-control, Tony rants at the diners in the prestigious restaurant: "You need me... I'm the bad guy... so, say goodbye to the bad guy ..." Self-pity is rarely so ugly as when practised by the successfully ambitious.

References: Tony begins by explaining that he learned to speak English by watching gangster movies "Humphrey Bogart... James Cagney." So, in the film's opening moments, De Palma pays tribute to the 30s Hollywood genre which, ironically, was about to revitalise his career. During this same sequence, one of the unseen cops asks Tony, "Do you like to dress up like a woman?" His denial underscores that we have moved on from *Dressed To Kill* into new, less psychologically complex territory. Tony and Frank sit in a mirrored booth in The Babylon nightclub. De Palma later employed similar booths for Fallow in *Bonfire Of The Vanities* and for Carlito in *Carlito's Way*. Although I'm not sure if it counts as a direct reference to Hitchcock – the master of suspense's movies were known, among many other things, for their unconvincing back-projections. Here, the driving scenes are always acted out against obvious back-projections. One of the few specific details which this film carries over from the 1932 version – is the sign saying 'The World Is Yours' at the foot of which, Tony will eventually die. The car chase, with the bomb under the lead car, and the children playing in it, combined with the dodgy back-projection, puts one in mind of the child on the bus with the bomb in the birdcage in Hitchcock's *Sabotage* (1936).

Artometer: 3/5

Body Double (1984)

The Cast: Craig Wasson (Jake Scully), Melanie Griffith[1] (Holly Body), Gregg Henry[2] (Sam), Deborah Shelton (Gloria Revelle), Dennis Franz[4] (Rubin)

The Crew: Director: Brian De Palma, Writers: Robert J Avrech & Brian De Palma, Producers: Brian De Palma & Howard Gottfried, Composer: Pino Donaggio,[5] Cinematographer: Stephen H Burum,[1] Editors: Gerald B Greenberg[3] & Bill Pankow[1]

The Plot: Jake Scully loses his job as a B-movie vampire, because he gets claustrophobic in the coffin. He goes home and finds his wife in bed with someone else. So, not a good day. At an audition, Sam, a similarly unemployed thesp, hears that Jake is looking for a place to stay, and offers him his apartment for a couple of weeks, while he's out of town. In said apartment, Sam shows Jake the home entertainment centre – a telescope – and points out which window to watch to see the neighbourhood's most beautiful exhibitionist undress and masturbate. Jake swiftly becomes obsessed with watching Gloria, then talks himself into believing she is being watched (by someone other than himself). The very next night, he sees her house burgled and watches impotently as she is brutally murdered. Now it falls to Jake to figure out who killed her and why, and exactly what his own part was in the crime.

The Thickening: Scarface earned De Palma the Hollywood reputation he had been striving for, even if it was a 'bad boy' reputation. But his desire to be acceptable and mainstream tugged against his desire to shock and play games with the Hollywood establishment. *Body Double* was his deliberate step back into Hitchcock territory.

The Themes. Violence: The sequence where the huge, conspicuously phallic drill is driven through Gloria, so that the bit continues through the floorboards to emerge from the ceiling below, whilst less gratuitous than, say, the chainsaw scene in *Scarface*, is still one of the nastier deaths De Palma has conceived.

Voyeurism/Surveillance: As Robert De Niro's character Jon had done, some 16 years previously, Jake settles down with his telescope for a night's entertainment watching a woman enjoying a 'private moment.'

The Motifs. Colours: This film opens with an obviously fake sunset – not greatly dissimilar to the ones in *Scarface*, or the one Carlito will fixate upon in *Carlito's Way*. This serves to set the film's overriding tone of things not necessarily being quite what they appear. Jake goes home to a typically white eighties home – and that's where he finds his girlfriend pulling the kinds of faces she never pulls when she's in bed with him. Well what does he expect, living in a white house in a De Palma movie. The very idea... Similarly, when he follows Gloria all around town, it never dawns on him that, since she's dressed all in white, she must mean trouble. When he breaks into her posh white house (whilst attempting to save her life) he is promptly attacked by her big white dog. Moments later he is sprayed with red blood from the gushing hole drilled through her body and through the bedroom floor.

Masks/Multiple Personas: 'Sam' manages to be himself and Alexander Revelle, Gloria's husband and, with the aid of a very conspicuous rubber mask, he is also 'The Indian.' In his case, this isn't because of a fractured personality, but as part of his devious plan to provide himself with a watertight alibi.

The Techniques. Stories Within Stories: In his improv class, he explains the origins of his claustrophobia lie with childhood trauma. His teacher tries to force him to break through the phobia but he isn't strong enough – he isn't sufficiently motivated. Yet. Susan Dworkin's *Double De Palma* reveals that this scene was inspired by an incident from De Palma's own childhood, when he was stuck behind a refrigerator when playing a game with his brothers.

Jake sees the neighbour dance again in a screen-in-screen, when he is watching the *Holly Does Hollywood* video trailer. The reason he recognises this pump and grind routine is, I suspect, because it is filmed from the same perspective as he last saw it - through a window.

When Jake is at the bottom of a grave, seemingly about to die from claustrophobic fright – Sam wisecracks that he needs another take and this time Jake should 'act' his way out of his fear. Jake promptly reverts to the moment his problems began, when he let his claustrophobia get the better of him on the movie set, and changes the way the situation came out. He fights his fear. Cut back to the present and his last and final chance to act on what he has learned.

The film ends as it began, with a shot from a horror movie. This time the 'magic' of movies is torn away (as it had been in *Blow Out*) by introducing the work that goes on between shots on a film set. It also explains, for those who hadn't cottoned on yet, what a 'body double' actually is.

Split-Screen: When Jake is peeping into the lingerie shop in that really unsuspicious way that is almost guaranteed to get your collar felt, he is shot with a split-dioptre, with him in focus in the distance, and the alarmed shop assistant in the foreground. Strangely, the sequence where Holly leaves Jake and attempts to flag down a lift, while he is desperately attempting to persuade the police to rescue her, is not presented in split-screen. One would have thought this would have been a textbook chance to employ the medium. The final overhead shot of the narrative is effectively a split-screen shot, with roaring, deadly water on one side of the line, and safe, solid earth on the other.

Long Takes/Tracking Shots: When Jake returns home, he can hear strange noises and proceeds, in a single tracking shot, through the seemingly endless labyrinth of his house to the bedroom.

References: As with *Blow Out*, this film begins within a B-movie-within-the-movie. Also, Jake's vampire costume and make-up in this sequence are in a similarly camp vein to Beef in *Phantom Of The Paradise*. Jake watching through a telescope, while his neighbour is being attacked is a direct lift from Hitchcock's *Rear Window* (1954). When Jake takes to following her around town, he is again emulating Jimmy Stewart, this time from *Vertigo* (1958). When Jake pursues 'The Indian' into a tunnel, he is attacked by his claustrophobia, which is presented visually by zooms and camera tilts, much as Stewart's attacks of vertigo are. When Gloria rescues him, their kiss is the rotating kiss from *Vertigo*, as borrowed by De Palma for the dances in *Obsession* and *Carrie*. The Vampire in the shower shot which runs under the end credits, is a reference back to *Dressed To Kill* where De Palma used the attack-in-the-shower motif twice; as well as to his own previous parodies of it in *Phantom* and *Blow Out*.

Artometer: 4/5

Wise Guys (1986)

The Cast: Danny DeVito (Harry Valentini), Joe Piscopo (Moe Dickstein), Harvey Keitel (Bobby Dilea), Ray Sharkey (Marco), Dan Hedaya (Anthony Castelo)

The Crew: Director: Brian De Palma, Writer: George Gallo, Producers: Patrick McCormick & Aaron and Irwin Russo, Composer: Ira Newborn, Cinematographer: Fred Schuler, Editor: Gerald B Greenberg[4]

The Plot: Harry is a small-time hood. Moe, his next-door neighbour is his dumb but well-meaning sidekick. Harry chooses to bet his boss Castelo's money on the wrong horse – and thereby loses $250,000. Since neither will tell him whose big idea it was, Castelo decides that the only way to get satisfaction from them, is to contract them to kill each other, then sit back and watch the fireworks. All the ingredients are there for a quick-fire black comedy. Unfortunately, they aren't mixed together to their best effect, making the film a tasteless concoction with little to recommend it.

The Thickening: With the possible exception of *Get To Know Your Rabbit* this, at least to my mind, marks the nadir of De Palma's career. It is a film almost entirely without charm, wit or his usual intelligence. Nevertheless, De Palma made it for a very precise reason – after his *Body Double* rebellion, he needed to show Hollywood that he could be a good boy and produce an uncontroversial studio film on time and on budget. As such, *Wise Guys* is an unqualified success since it cemented his position as a player in Hollywood. I remain unconvinced that the end justified these means.

The Motifs. Colours: You know things are going to take a turn for the better, when they arrive in a casino hotel, with a lobby decorated in gaudy red. When Moe turns uncharacteristically violent at the film's crescendo – he wears the obligatory white suit.

Doubles: The film begins with Harry preening himself in his mirror, as the camera pulls back, we see little Harry Jnr doing exactly the same thing in front of *his* mirror. Then, when Harry wanders downstairs, his breakfast with his wife perfectly mirrors Moe's morning with his mother. They even leave their houses at the same moment. Harry and Moe are binary opposites when it comes to relating to the Mob. Moe is a good Jewish boy who is desperate to sully his reputation and make it as a big-time hood. Harry, on the other hand, being Italian, is trapped into a life of organised crime but has aspirations of becoming legit for the sake of his son. Later, their aspirations are turned on them when Mr Castelo turns them against each other – each trying to do the opposite thing, for the same reason.

Slow/Fast-Moe: When Harry is preparing to start the engine on Castelo's potentially booby-trapped car, the camera pans around very slowly as the entire street clears - everyone running at an accelerated pace – until there is just him and the car. Mr Castelo's reaction to learning precisely what has happened to his money, is presented in suitably melodramatic slow motion.

Split-Screen: When Mr Castelo has driven a wedge between the life-long friends, they return home and, symbolising the chasm which has now opened between them, De Palma shoots them with a split-dioptre lens – pushing Moe way back into the background, whilst bringing Harry right into the foreground.

References: The opening line of dialogue is "You talking to me?" In the traditional manner, this line is delivered to a mirror. This is De Palma tipping a wink to his long-time friends Scorsese and De Niro and their career-defining film *Taxi Driver* (1976). Mr Castelo eats with a huge fish tank behind him. As well as proving useful in extracting information from the unforthcoming, this tank is also a visual precursor to the aquarium restaurant sequence in *Mission:Impossible*. Harvey Keitel's performance as Bobby Dilea, the smiling, well-mannered fixer, is a dry run for his similar (although far more successful) performance as Mr Wolf in *Pulp Fiction* (1994). When Moe is sitting in one of the hotel's circular baths, he evokes Tony's much larger, grander bath in *Scarface*.

Artometer: 2/5

The Untouchables (1987)

The Cast: Kevin Costner (Eliot Ness), Sean Connery (Jim Malone), Robert De Niro[4] (Al Capone), Charles Martin Smith (Oscar Wallace), Andy Garcia (George Stone), Billy Drago (Nitti)

The Crew: Director: Brian De Palma, Writer: David Mamet, Books: Oscar Fraley & Eliot Ness & Paul Robsky, Producers: Ray Hartwick & Art Linson,[1] Composer: Ennio Morricone,[1] *I Pagliacci* by Ruggero Leoncavallo, Cinematographer: Stephen H Burum[2]. Editors: Gerald B Greenberg[5] & Bill Pankow[2]

The Plot: Eliot Ness is an idealistic, ambitious young G-Man, given the task of cleaning up the streets of Chicago. He assembles a gang of unlikely but incorruptible heroes to help him with this. Through resolution, brutality and due process (but not necessarily in that order) Eliot takes on the king of Chicago, Al Capone, in the closest thing 'civilised' America is going to get to a high noon shoot-out.

The Thickening: Although *Wise Guys* is an almost entirely ignored film now, it served a crucial purpose in De Palma's career. It proved he could be uncontroversial. He could make a studio movie without kicking up a fuss, and without producing something dripping with blood. Now he had proved himself... again... Hollywood felt it was ready to trust him with something completely mainstream, inoffensive and uncomplicated: *The Untouchables*.

The Themes. Violence: The traditional dark red De Palmanian blood belches out across the dining table, when Capone pummels one of his capos to death with a bat. This is the first sign we see of the Capone that Ness wants to put away, previously we've only seen the grinning darling of the tabloids. Capone is obsessed with the Wild West idea of the showdown. He constantly demands to be faced "like a man," yet he employs others to do most of his killing for him. When Ness can't get Capone's man to surrender, he has to shoot him, then demands "Is this a game?" Well, after a fashion, yes. It's a game of one-upmanship. Who can kill the most ruthlessly and effectively? To intimidate their prisoner, Malone holds Ness' recent kill against a wall, yells at it, then shoots it. This is particularly effective, since the prisoner doesn't know the victim was already too dead to care. Ironically, it is not this type of macho posturing, or the gunplay which brings Capone down, but simple, boring accountancy. By throwing Nitti off the roof, Ness breaks the cycle of gunplay. He can walk away from 'the game' with no actual blood on his hands.

The Motifs: Possibly to better represent the period in which the film is set – a time when films were (almost) all in black and white – De Palma resists employing his usual colour palette too much, concentrating instead on making this film visually very formal. It's a very flat and angular world Eliot lives in. We get lots of straight-on shots of square windows and rectangular doors. There's a lot of straight-on shots of architectural features like bridges and buildings. Generally speaking, when the camera moves, it moves sideways, such as in the house out in the field, where the camera tracks from outside on the veranda, to inside.

Colours: The assassin, Nitti, is accompanied by Morricone's harmonica, underscoring that he is a bad guy in the traditional Wild West sense. Despite the fact he is dressed all in white, this is a De Palma film, and white is a colour to be energetically avoided.

The cops wear black uniforms, the gangsters white uniforms. The traditional good guy/bad guy aesthetic of the Hollywood cowboy film has been turned on its head. But then, since the cops are, without significant exception, corrupt, they blacken the meaning of their uniforms simply by wearing them. Indeed, when Nitti breaks in to the inner sanctum, he does so in the uniform of a cop. The Untouchables are a new idea, they exist outside the normal order of things, consequently they have no colour code and no uniform.

When Malone fights the corrupt police chief, they are bathed in red light. The threats Malone issues in this fight are the direct cause of his death. When Ness arrives at his house, he follows the trail of vivid red blood to his friend's side.

Masks/Multiple Personas: Capone purports to be a respectable businessman, and jokes with the press who adore him. But, behind the scenes he is a single-minded thug content to kill anyone who won't sell him their soul. Under his influence, morality and the law become meaningless, save that they serve his purpose. He is very far from just a respectable businessman.

To make right right and wrong wrong again, Ness must begin by reversing his own standards and his own beliefs. Finally, he accepts that, to bring The Chicago Way to an end, he has to play by its rules until Capone is sent down. As he says: "I have become what I beheld, and I am content that I have done right."

The Techniques. POV: The one sequence of POV in this film, begins, as these sequences so frequently do with De Palma, outside a window. Then we climb in and proceed, still from the assassin's point of view, along Malone's corridor

Slow/Fast-Mo: The mother with the pram, making agonising progress up the stairs, seems to be in slow motion even before it is. The moments draw on torturously long, before Ness decides to give up his vantage point and help her. Then, as soon as he is recognised, everything switches to slow motion. The pram bumps back down the steps, the only sounds we hear are gunshots and the baby crying.

Long Takes/Tracking Shots: Capone and Ness are both introduced with long takes where they are addressing the press. Capone is listened to respectfully, as he reasons that it is better, in Chicago, to do business with a kind word and a gun. This scene is seen from above, with Capone relaxed and ebullient. Ness' press conference is seen from the perspective of the crowd, who jabber over each other and don't really listen to his answers. He's the new boy in town. Capone has always been there, and probably always will be, so why should they worry too much about the police's latest failed attempt to beat him?

The sequence of hunting Malone in his own house, all seen in one long take from the killer's perspective, then the same journey again as we follow Malone, spilling his guts all over his carpet is, in my opinion, the most perfectly realised use of one of De Palma's favourite techniques. To add operatic tragedy to this scene, it is accompanied by the soundtrack from *I Pagliacci*.

References: Ennio Morricone's hypnotic opening theme, is a reworking of his theme for Gillo Pontecorvo's *The Battle Of Algiers* (1965), a film which concerns the battle of right against wrong, for political ends. There are also tell-tale traces of the harmonica last used in the Leone spaghetti westerns, underscoring the contention that Chicago under the thumb of the Italian gangsters was, at least in terms of law and order, not greatly dissimilar to the frontier towns of the Wild West. The little girl picking up the bomb and hurrying to return it to the bomber – is an indirect reference to Hitchcock's *Sabotage* (1936) which had a boy on a bus with a bomb. It also establishes early on that children are cannon fodder in this film, which adds to the tension of the later *Battleship Potemkin* (1925) reference, where the pram rattles down the stair whilst bullets fly around it. Also, note how the dates of both of these references are roughly appropriate to the period setting. The notorious 'enthusiasms' scene, with the banqueting table and the baseball bat, is lifted almost intact from Roger Corman's *The St Valentine's Day Massacre* (1967), where Jason Robards played Capone. As with several of the key moments in this film, the shoot-out between Ness and Nitti takes place on a staircase. In this case it's a spiral staircase, shot to resemble the one in *Vertigo*.

Artometer: 3/5

Casualties Of War (1989)

The Cast: Michael J Fox (Eriksson), Sean Penn[1] (Meserve), Thuy Thu Le (Oahn), Don Harvey (Clark), John C Reilly (Hatcher), John Leguizamo[1] (Diaz), Ving Rhames[1] (Lieutenant Reilly), Dale Dye[1] (Captain Hill)

The Crew: Director: Brian De Palma, Writer: David Rabe, Based on journalism of Daniel Lang, Producers: Fred C Caruso[3] & Art Linson,[2] Composer: Ennio Morricone,[2] Cinematographer: Stephen H Burum,[3] Editor: Bill Pankow[3]

The Plot: Eriksson is a new recruit (or 'cherry') in the jungles of Nam. One of his unit Sergeants, Browning, is killed. They are all terribly shocked by the sudden death of this "armour plated" short-timer. The surviving sergeant, Meserve, a man far too young and unpredictable to be trusted with authority, decides that his men deserve a treat. So, when they are sent out on a long-range recon mission, they visit one of the local villages and kidnap a young girl to take along as "portable R'n'R." Eriksson is not alone in being unhappy about this, but Meserve's control is so strong, that Eriksson is the only one who refuses to rape her and then, back at camp, he is the only one who complains. So he has to face the threats of his colleagues, the indifference of his commanding officers, and his own guilt ...

The Thickening: The success of *The Untouchables* at the box office made De Palma a Hollywood player. De Palma had craved the money and power of mainstream Hollywood and after 20 years it was within his grasp. Then he decided to make a big, expensive but deeply personal film he'd been wanting to make for many years. He knew this would be a gamble, because to alienate Hollywood again could put him out in the cold forever.

De Palma's trademark motifs and techniques are hardly used in this film. He didn't want to insert an overt Hitchcock reference, for example, and throw the viewer back out of the film. He wanted us to be as trapped by this horror story as his characters are. In this way, *Casualties* is De Palma's least playful and most heart-felt movie.

The Themes. Manipulation: Eriksson and Diaz are deeply troubled about what they are being party to, but they are soldiers, it is not their place to question orders. When Eriksson does question Meserve about it, he is punished by being put on point – the most dangerous position when out in the field. Diaz is the first one to actually air his concerns out loud: "If I don't wanna mess with her, man, do I hafta?" Yet, when it comes down to it, he hasn't got the character to support Eriksson and be an outcast from his team. In an attempt to reinforce his authority, Meserve insists that Eriksson kills Oahn, despite the fact that Clark is keen to do it. Eriksson refuses, so then Meserve orders Diaz. "Don't let him make you do it, Diaz!" Begs Eriksson. So the situation has developed into a battle of wills between Meserve and Eriksson. When he thinks she is escaping, Meserve's need to control his men is such that he has to keep on yelling "Shoot her" when it would be far simpler and quicker for him to turn his own gun on her. Back at base, his superiors try to persuade Eriksson to drop his charges, then they threaten him.

Violence: After the intensity of the rape sequence, the viewer could be forgiven for wishing a quick death upon Oahn yet, when it comes, it is a typically De Palmanian brutal and slow death, as she staggers along the railway line, blood pouring from her wounds.

The Motifs. Colours: The red light in the VC tunnel throws deep black shadows, which make it look like hell. When they are searching the village for the 'right' girl, they are using a torch with a red light bulb. During *Dressed To Kill*'s climactic nightmare, the asylum was saturated in a deep, penetrating blue. After the rape in *Casualties Of War*, the rain cascades down and dowses everything in a similarly nightmarish blue.

Doubles: When Meserve is trying to explain the failure of his colleagues to make any impact on the hearts and minds of the locals, he puts it down to their confusion over what is right and wrong: "They confused themselves if they Cong or they not Cong!" "Yeah, they're schizophrenic, man!" Eriksson tries to relate to them, to make friends, but the short-timers are far more cynical than him. They don't see the Vietnamese as people, anymore.

Ultimately, redemption is offered to Eriksson when he returns the scarf to the woman who is Oahn 's double. She states, matter-of-factly: "You had a bad dream, didn't you. It's over now, I think." Unfortunately, it wasn't just a dream and it isn't over that simply; as was demonstrated by *The Visitors* (1971, dir Elia Kazan), which was also inspired by Daniel Lang's coverage of this incident. The Kazan version, rather than detailing the crime and court martial, speculated on the retribution which may very well have taken place when everyone made it back to America.

The Techniques. POV: The hunt through the village to find the best-looking girl to take, is seen entirely from their point of view, deliberately implicating us, the viewers, in their abuse.

During the extensive repeated rape sequence, the camera is dutched (tilted slightly to one side) to give the image a slightly unworldly appearance. We see everything from a static position, from Eriksson's perspective, and from a safe distance away. All of this is to serve as a distancing device so that we, the viewer, aren't drawn too far in. After all, implicating your audience in voyeurism, as De Palma often does, is one thing, involving them in a rape is something else entirely.

Stories Within Stories: The opening shot of the film features, among other things, a man sitting on a train reading a paper with the headline 'Nixon Resigning.' This dates the film squarely at the very end of the period which is now mostly remembered for Vietnam and for political corruption. Eriksson, who is also sitting on the train, drifts off to sleep and into a memory flashback which forms the ensuing film.

Split-Screen: To illustrate the underground tunnels, De Palma built a cutaway set, so that the camera could start with Eriksson above ground, show him fall, then move smoothly underground to show his legs kicking and thrashing in the tunnel. A similar cutaway set was built for the inside-outside shot of the cabin in the field in *The Untouchables*, and the elevator shaft in *Mission:Impossible*. This sequence continues with a parallel narrative of Meserve hunting for Eriksson above ground, while the tunnel-rat approaches him from below ground. When the men are in their billet preparing for R'n'R, Meserve is in the extreme foreground, unseen by them, eavesdropping on their conversation, shaving himself and seemingly suffering immense, barely restrained emotional trauma. Perhaps the death of his partner, Browning, is one atrocity too many for him. Maybe this is the point where he snaps. Whilst Eriksson is distracted, fighting for his life against the VC on the shore below, De Palma employed a split-dioptre shot to show Clark knifing the girl in the background

References: Whether by accident or design, Oliver Stone almost stole De Palma's thunder with his 1986 movie *Platoon*, which employed the ad-line 'The First Casualty Of War Is Innocence.' The script for *Casualties Of War* (the title having been taken from Lang's original article) had been doing the rounds in Hollywood for decades, and it was no secret that De Palma was determined to bring it to the screen one day. The riverside railway line bears a striking resemblance to the main location of *The Bridge On The River Kwai* (1957), De Palma's favourite film. The nightmare out in the field cuts back into the hospital through an image borrowed from *Apocalypse Now* (1979) of helicopter rotor-blades turning into a rotating overhead fan.

Artometer: 5/5

The Nineties: Shake Hands With The Devil

The Bonfire Of The Vanities (1990)

The Cast: Tom Hanks (Sherman McCoy), Bruce Willis (Peter Fallow), Melanie Griffith[2] (Maria Ruskin), Saul Rubinek (Jed Kramer), Morgan Freeman (Judge White), F Murray Abraham[2] (Abe Weiss, uncredited), Geraldo Rivera (Robert Corso, uncredited)

The Crew: Director: Brian De Palma, Writer: Michael Cristofer, Novel: Tom Wolfe, Producers: Fred C Caruso[4] & Brian De Palma & others, Composer: Dave Grusin, Cinematographer: Vilmos Zsigmond,[3] Editors: Bill Pankow[4] & David Ray[2]

The Plot: Almost everybody believes that 'Master Of The Universe' and über-yuppie, Sherman McCoy, is invincible. Yet, in the film's opening moments, he attempts to ring his girlfriend Maria, but accidentally dials his own number and ends up talking to his wife. How very vincible. Similarly, when distracted by Maria's heavy petting, he drives down the wrong off-ramp, then she runs over a black youth (who may or may not have been about to mug them). Suddenly, a media and political circus is built up around the big story of the multi-millionaire wünderkind and the poor black boy he crippled. So, it falls to alcoholic reporter Peter Fallow to save McCoy's bacon.

The Thickening: In need of a guaranteed success after the flop of the highly-personal *Casualties*, De Palma signed on for *Bonfire*. Unfortunately, pressurised by the studio into working without a producer, ambushed time and again by the New York authorities and pressure groups during the filming, hampered by some dubious casting decisions (of stars rather than actors) and ridiculed by a vicious media-wide hate campaign, the film never really stood a chance. Nevertheless, it contains some bravura De Palma moments, and one can only wonder at what delights the original 30-minute-longer cut held before antagonistic preview audiences and the studio forced their opinions on it. Today, the film serves as an interesting snapshot of late-eighties Hollywood. Also, it is fascinating to watch the Hanks and Willis screen personas in transition. They were both moderately-successful comedians at the time, and were soon to become extraordinarily successful big shots.

The Themes. Voyeurism/Surveillance: We are introduced to Sherman voyeuristically, looking down into his house through a rain-lashed skylight, before moving in to find out what is going on. Later, Sherman's freedom is won, because of his conversation with Maria which is recorded illicitly by the landlords of her building, in an attempt to prove she is committing rent fraud.

The Motifs. Colours: The drama here turns on the ignorance and mutual-mistrust felt by whites for blacks and blacks for whites. As he demonstrated in *Hi Mom!*, the issue of colour in society is never simply black and white. Both the leaders of the white and black communities are tainted with their own greedy agendas. When Don Giovanni is dragged into hell, this is symbolised by red lights and prison doors being slammed shut. When McCoy is dragged into prison, the doors slam shut in front of him and the lighting turns red.

Doubles: Fallow's career is the reverse of McCoy's. As he, himself puts it: "Sherman lost everything, but gained his soul. Whereas I, you see, who started with so little, gained everything."

When Sherman has his 'touching' reconciliation with his father, the moulding around the door behind them, is identical to that behind the judge's chair when he is giving his pompous "Go home and be decent" speech. Ironically, this connects Sherman's decision to perjure himself and his straight-as-a-die father's acceptance of this, with the judge's invocation of good American values.

Masks/Multiple Personas: Fallow is a character with a changing persona. This is implied on the several occasions we see him reflected in mirrors, suggesting he is a man with two faces. When he finally meets McCoy, he feels sympathy for the man he has brought low, and so turns his talents to redeeming McCoy and, indirectly, himself. "My little encounter with the real Sherman McCoy was spoiling everything. The truth has a way of doing that."

The various television reporters and the leaders they interview, particularly the Reverend Bacon, also display two faces – one for their public and the cameras, one in private.

Stories Within Stories: The whole story is told as a sustained flashback by Peter Fallow. Within this, we have the parallel story of Don Giovanni's descent into hell.

The Techniques. POV: When Kramer goes to see the fearsome Reverend Bacon, the sequence is shot almost entirely from Kramer's point of view, with the Reverend staring intimidatingly straight into his/our eyes.

Slow/Fast-Mo: The film begins with a time-lapse bird's-eye view of New York. This was the brainchild of Second Unit Director, Eric Schwab, who spent weeks scouting buildings and negotiating with their owners, in an attempt to find a shot De Palma would admit was better than he could have done himself.

There was originally to be a riot in the courtroom after Sherman presents his tape, which would result in him rescuing Judge White and running, in slow motion, through the mélée, swinging the sword of justice from a fallen statue. After the first bad previews, this scene was re-cut to run at normal speed, then cut out altogether.

Split-Screen: The single sequence of split-screen here shows Geraldo Rivera interviewing Reverend Bacon whilst Fallow looks on. We see what goes on behind the scenes, and contrast it with what goes on in front of the camera. The division is not sufficiently marked to make the distinction between the lies on the left of the screen and the truth on the right entirely clear. The technique, therefore, seems wasted.

Long Takes/Tracking Shots: After the rapid time-lapse of a day in the life of New York, the film proper begins with a 4-minute tracking shot of Willis arriving for a press conference in an underground car-park, making his way down corridors, through crowds, into an elevator, through a change of clothes and ultimately into the flashback that is the film.

References: The introduction to McCoy, looking down through his rain-lashed skylight, is a reference to Welles' celebrated through-the-glass shot in *Citizen Kane*, as well as to De Palma's previous use of same in *Phantom* and *Dressed To Kill* among other films. Fallow works for the New York tabloid, *City Lights*, named after Chaplin's 1931 film about simple human decency in the heart of a great cruel city. When McCoy sees the 2 black youths approaching, De Palma employs the disorienting 'double-reverse' shot which Hitchcock devised to demonstrate James Stewart's vertigo in *Vertigo* (1958) and Spielberg rediscovered for *Jaws* (1975). When Kramer walks the corridors of power discussing the mysterious Bronx hit and run, the lengthy reverse tracking shot reminds one of any number of Kubrick shots but most obviously that of Kirk Douglas patrolling the trenches in *Paths Of Glory* (1957). When Fallow meets Mr Ruskin, it is in a booth in a restaurant with a mirrored wall behind it, just like Tony Montana and Frank Lopez's favourite booth in *Scarface*. Let's face it, this whole damn story is just John Landis' *Trading Places* (1983) without the jokes. The shot of the umbrellas scuttling down the courthouse steps is a visual reference to Hitchcock's similarly rain-soaked *Foreign Correspondent* (1940).

Artometer: 2/5

Raising Cain (1992)

The Cast: John Lithgow[3] (Carter/Cain/Dr Nix/Josh/Margo), Lolita Davidovich (Jenny), Steven Bauer[2] (Jack), Frances Sternhagen (Dr Waldheim), Gregg Henry[3] (Lieutenant Terri)

The Crew: Writer/Director: Brian De Palma, Producers: Gale Anne Hurd & Michael R Joyce, Composer: Pino Donaggio,[6] Cinematographer: Stephen H Burum,[4] Editors: Paul Hirsch[8] & Robert Dalva & Bonnie Koehler

The Plot: Carter Nix is a deeply troubled man. A tragic figure, his personality was fractured by his mad professor father, who abused and tortured him throughout his childhood simply to see whether or not he could deliberately manufacture a multiple personality. Desperate to help his resurrected father (who may or may not be a figment of his imagination) Carter sets about kidnapping children and murdering their mothers, to give his father fresh new minds to destroy. As he falls further into this madness, his control over his alternative personalities slips and more and more psychopathic sides to him are revealed.

The Thickening: Treading much the same ground as *Dressed To Kill*, this film seems to draw a line under De Palma's 'Hitchcockian' phase, which began 21 years earlier with *Sisters*. From here on, De Palma put his grasp of visual grammar to very different uses.

The Themes. Manipulation: Cain bullies Carter into giving in and letting him take over. This could, in very basic Freudian terms, be seen as the empowering Ego quelling the qualms of the Superego, before going off and committing the distasteful act which the Id demands. Carter allows himself to be bullied and, indeed, utterly subjugated by his other selves because this sort of abuse is all he has ever known. His father manipulated him with drugs and psychological torture.

Violence: The violence here is all fairly bloodless. Chloroformed handkerchiefs, that sort of thing. De Palma constantly plays games with our expectations of him. Jenny suffers a spectacular and nasty death, impaled on the spear of a statue. This is the sort of death we expect from a De Palma movie. Then, suddenly, she is awake and it was all a dream. Relax. He's tricked us. Yet, moments later, Carter does murder her with a pillow over her face. Then he loads her into the back of a car and sinks it into a swamp. As it goes down, she revives, just in time to drown. Possibly. Without a drop of blood being spilled, this is one of De Palma's cruellest and most protracted deaths and then, at the end of it, you're still not sure if she's gone.

Voyeurism/Surveillance: Since this is the tale of a man who has been under surveillance and parental manipulation all his life, it is appropriate that the film begins with an image from a closed-circuit TV monitor of Nix talking to his daughter in bed. Jenny's guilty secret is that Jack's wife died of shock when she saw Jack and Jenny kissing. When she is having sex with Jack, she imagines being watched. This is her guilt manifesting itself, or is it? Did she see Carter watching her, or didn't she? We'll have to wait for the rerun to find out.

The Motifs. Colours: Although this is a film almost entirely without blood, and with very little of the obvious colour-coding which has been particularly common through De Palma's eighties films, this film finishes with the image of Margo, dressed in red, emerging from behind Jenny.

Implying a violent tussle over 'motherhood' of their child, but not actually showing it. As 'shock' endings go, this is at least as effective as *Carrie*, and far more effective than *The Fury*.

Masks/Multiple Personas: Carter/Cain is the clearest and most numerous case of fractured identity De Palma has yet dealt with. Cain turns up whenever Carter is suffering stress. He is the empowerer, the facilitator. Through his abuse, Jenny's entire personality alters from the guilt-ridden and harmless to vengeful and motivated.

The Techniques. POV: When the multiple personalities talk to each other, they address the camera directly, thereby making us the other half of their conversation. Only fair, I suppose, since there's no one else in the room. After Jenny's story, the tale rewinds and we see the whole day again, from Carter's perspective as he spies on her. When his fears of infidelity are proven, he 'leaves' and allows Cain to take over. Later, when Jenny reappears, she makes her dramatic entrance staring directly at us, through her baby-surveillance camera.

Slow/Fast-Mo: The entire elevator/pram/sundial showdown is played out in slow motion, to extend the tension, especially when the baby falls to (un)certain death on the concrete below.

Split-Screen: Quoting the sequence from *Dressed To Kill* where Peter sits in the foreground eavesdropping on the police in the background, we get Nix in the background with a sketch artist, whilst the old cop in the foreground is revealing the backstory of evil Dr Nix.

Long Takes/Tracking Shots: Waldheim's backstory, explaining Dr Nix's madness, is detailed in one immensely elaborate take covering 3 levels, several flights of stairs, one elevator, lots of corridors and about four and a half minutes; during which time Frances Sternhagen delivers what must be one of the longest monologues in cinema history. Lithgow gets to do some grandstanding of his own when, under Waldheim's cross-examination, he manifests 2 of his alternate personalities, in an extended shot as the camera slowly dollies round the seated characters.

References: This film takes its title from *Raising Kane*, a book written by De Palma's favourite critic, Pauline Kael, about the making of one De Palma's favourite films, *Citizen Kane* (1941). Jenny's dalliance with Jack, cunningly plays with the same scenario De Palma used in *Dressed To Kill*. Since we all know what happened to Kate after her infidelity in that film, De Palma uses that knowledge against us, constantly threatening to have Jenny killed, then not following through. Locking Jenny into a car and sinking it into a swamp is also Norman Bates' modus operandi in *Psycho* (1960). The name of the female personality, Margo, relates right back to *Murder À La Mod*, as it was the name of the character who is murdered in 3 different ways. It also relates to Margot Kidder, who played the divided personality in *Sisters*. The game show in *Sisters* was named after Michael Powell's much-maligned movie *Peeping Tom* (1960 – the same year *Psycho* was released). De Palma returns to that film for inspiration now, since it featured a young man, Mark, who had been driven mad by his father's fear experiments. The scene with the elevator evokes *Dressed To Kill* because it features a homicidal man dressed as a woman, then moves into a quote of the Odessa Steps sequence from *Battleship Potemkin*, with the pram rolling into harms way.

Artometer: 4/5

Carlito's Way (1993)

The Cast: Al Pacino[2] (Carlito Brigante), Sean Penn[2] (David Kleinfeld), Penelope Ann Miller (Gail), Luis Guzman[1] (Pachanga), John Leguizamo[2] (Benny Blanco)

The Crew: Director: Brian De Palma, Writer: David Koepp[1], Novels: *Carlito's Way* & *After Hours* by Edwin Torres, Producers: Martin Bregman[2] & Louis A Stroller[4] & others, Composer: Patrick Doyle, *Lakmé* by Léo Delibes, Cinematographer: Stephen H Burum,[5] Editors: Bill Pankow[5] & Kristina Boden

The Plot: Carlito Brigante is an underworld legend but, after 5 years inside, he has had time to think and reassess and has decided that his drug-pushing, gun-toting days are behind him. He's going to gather some money then go off and live on a paradise island and sell cars. Something boring. Something safe. Unfortunately, Carlito's lawyer, Kleinfeld has, in his absence, become a big and ruthless player. As Carlito is trying to clean up his act, Kleinfeld is getting correspondingly dirtier. Eventually Carlito learns that you can never escape your past. The faster you crawl out of hell, the harder the demons try to drag you back in.

The Thickening: This is De Palma's first film noir. Essentially, the noir protagonist is a character with too much past and not enough future. Redemption is only achievable with death, because only with the full payment of all outstanding debts can the books be cleared. In essence, Carlito is dead before the film begins. As he tells Kleinfeld, "I was dead and buried and you dug me up!" Consequently, he is now living on borrowed time. He has been given a chance to undo some of the evils of his life, but he fails. His time is wasted.

The Themes. Manipulation: Kleinfeld's story begins with him being manipulated by someone he has stolen a million from – a man who, despite his incarceration, can very easily have the lawyer killed if he doesn't arrange a jailbreak. Turning the manipulation around, Kleinfeld brings Carlito in on his little plan because, as Carlito had rashly stated "I owe you my life!" Now it is time for the lawyer to cash in that debt.

Voyeurism/Surveillance: The reason Carlito is freed after 5 years of a life sentence is because it transpires that the surveillance tapes which sent him down were acquired illegally. Lalin, the "stand-up guy" who now must use a wheelchair, is sent to tempt Carlito back into his criminal ways, but Carlito is wise and Lalin is wired. The same prosecutor who used illegal tapes to trap Carlito, now attempts to use the same technique to persuade Carlito to turn Kleinfeld over. His final threat is ominously appropriate; "You think you're going to sail off into the sunset – think again!"

The Motifs. Colours: Throughout this film, Carlito wears black. Ordinarily this is the colour of the bad guy, but not in a De Palma film. Unlike when Pacino played Tony Montana, this time he isn't 'the bad guy.' This time he is, for want of a more accurate description: 'the anti-hero,' and this is demonstrated in his choice of black clothing.

The opening scene is in black and white, except for the billboard of an orange sunset, decorated with the label 'Paradise.' Here, in the film's opening seconds, De Palma is binding this film to *Scarface*, the last of De Palma's films to dwell on orange sunsets and concepts of paradise, either on Earth or off it.

Carlito is immediately sucked back into his old world, when he agrees to go with his little brother on a drug-money drop. This is after he has sagely advised Kleinfeld that "A favour gonna kill you faster than a bullet." One of Carlito's many flaws is that he doesn't listen to his own advice. They arrive at the pool hall in a red car and, once inside, we immediately notice that the hall has red walls. Once more, he has been drawn into his own version of hell. The outcome is inevitably bloody. Unable to resist the temptation of the money left by the dead drug pushers, he takes it and, with that decision, his fate is sealed.

Even though he sinks the money into the nightspot El Paraiso and intends to make just enough money to move to Paradise Island, he has been to hell and made a pact. There will be no paradise for Carlito. On his first night in charge, he meets Benny Blanco, who wears a vivid red suit, symbolic of the violence he is going to bring into Carlito's life. When he tussles with Benny, over 'ownership' of the escort Steffi, he throws him out of his club from a red-walled antechamber. But he no longer has the will to have Benny killed. As he correctly surmises in his voice-over, "Bad move... the street is watching." Benny will pick his moment, and come back.

The street is a violent red place, but the real power, the real corruption, is not down at street level. When we see Kleinfeld's beach-side property, we begin to understand - everyone wears white. The buildings are white, as is the furniture and the umbrellas and even the sand. White, as we know, generally means evil in a De Palma movie. And there sits Carlito, surrounded by it.

Out in the ocean, in Kleinfeld's big white boat, the murder of Tony the escaping villain is bathed in the saturated blue we have seen during moments of nightmarish violence in *Casualties* and *Dressed To Kill*. Indeed, this is the moment where Carlito's dream becomes a nightmare, and Gail's nightmare comes that bit closer to becoming true.

Back on the street, when Carlito is fleeing for his life, he takes a trip on a red tube train, then hides behind a red pillar.

Doubles: In one important respect, Carlito is the exact opposite of Tony Montana – he is a man who will be brought low by his lack of ambition. Because he doesn't want to play the get-rich-quick game, he hangs around too long and runs out of his borrowed time.

In the nightclub, he watches a woman dance and this reminds him of Gail, his lost love. It is Gail's silhouette he sees pirouetting on the beach in his fantasy paradise.

Masks/Multiple Personas: Gail refers to Carlito as 'Charlie' throughout. But 'Charlie' is the man he can never be. The safe and respectable man. The man he so desperately wants to be, if his past would let him.

The Techniques. POV: The film begins with Carlito's perspective on his own assassination. People crowd around him, lift him onto a stretcher and then, as if in an out-of-body experience, we look down and we can see Carlito, as well as hear his thoughts. When Carlito moves into El Paraiso, which he hopes will be his salvation, we first see it through his eyes.

Slow/Fast-Mo: The assassination is in slow motion, as Carlito has time to register what has happened to him, has time to let his recent life flash before our eyes, and then has time to make peace with himself and his dreams of paradise. Now, maybe, he is going to a different kind of paradise. The second time we see it, we have a context, we know who some of the faces are. We know Carlito's time has run out.

Stories Within Stories: The entire narrative is a flashback, as Carlito recounts the last few weeks of his life which have brought him to this decisive moment. Gail looks in the mirror and tells Carlito her fear: "I know how this dream ends ..." then she describes the death she expects for him, which is exactly what we saw at the beginning of the film.

Long Takes/Tracking Shots: When Carlito leaves Kleinfeld's hospital room, an extended tracking shot follows him to the elevator, then returns to follow Vinnie, the assassin, as he goes back up the corridor to Kleinfeld's room. When Carlito is evading Vinnie in Grand Central, he ducks and dives round corners and along walls and finally down an escalator, all in one take.

References: As the billboard with the orange sunset on it links Carlito to the young, ambitious Tony Montana, so does his "Look at me, in a club, playing Humphrey Bogart!" Carlito's pursuit of Gail is similar to the obsessive behaviour in Hitchcock's *Vertigo* and De Palma's *Obsession* and *Body Double*. When Carlito stands and watches Gail (as so many De Palmanian characters have stood outside and looked at their loves through rain-lashed windows) the Herrmannesque music is replaced by the even more plaintive strains of Delibes' *Lakmé*. The assassination attempt on Kleinfeld refers back to elevator violence in *Dressed To Kill* and *The Untouchables*, since he is stabbed when awaiting a lift. The film's showdown takes place, as with *Blow Out* and *The Untouchables*, in a railway station – clearly one of De Palma's favourite locales. The shoot-out on the stairs resembles *The Untouchables*, with just a touch of *Scarface*'s staircase showdown thrown in for good measure.

Artometer: 3/5

Mission: Impossible (1996)

The Cast: Tom Cruise (Ethan Hunt), Jon Voight (Jim Phelps), Emmanuelle Béart (Claire Phelps), Kristin Scott Thomas (Sarah Davies), Emilio Estevez (Jack Harmen, uncredited), Jean Reno (Franz Krieger), Ving Rhames[2] (Luther Stickell), Vanessa Redgrave (Max), Dale Dye[2] (Frank Barnes)

The Crew: Director: Brian De Palma, Writers: David Koepp[2] & Robert Towne & Steven Zaillian, Producers: Tom Cruise & Paula Wagner & Paul Hitchcock, Composer: Danny Elfman, *Theme To Mission:Impossible* by Lalo Schifrin, Cinematographer: Stephen H Burum,[6] Editor: Paul Hirsch[9]

The Plot: The Impossible Mission Force are all killed off, except for their 'point man' Ethan Hunt. He sets out to find who double-crossed his team, and gets involved in some impossible high jinks on the way. And the critics say that this film was complicated!

The Thickening: This was De Palma's first dalliance with the kind of massive-budget no-brain summer-spectacular which have become the stock-in-trade of his best friend Steven Spielberg. Although De Palma's track-record has become more consistent than many of his contemporaries, for decades he had been bemoaning the fact that he had never really made a huge hit movie. Well, he has now!

The Themes. Violence: Given this film's predilection for observation and surveillance, it is not inappropriate that the first casualty (Jack) should die by being impaled in the eyes.

Voyeurism/Surveillance: This is a film very much about surveillance and observation. It begins with an image refilmed off a closed-circuit television screen of Ethan, in disguise, pumping a suspect for information. All IMF missions take place under complete supervision and surveillance. The camera in the spectacles that all the agents wear is the culmination of 30 years of personal surveillance techniques. All of the various remote camera, telephoto lenses and miniature microphones have been leading to this. When Ethan, jittery and panicked, rings Kittridge to report the loss of his team, his first thought is still of possible surveillance: "Are we secure?"

The Motifs. Colours: Colours are reversed here. In this film, white is good and black is bad. Who'd'a thunk it?

Masks/Multiple Personas: Cruise is introduced pulling off one of his rubber masks, which are far more convincing than, say the one worn by Sam in *Body Double*, because modern computerised morphing technology allows one actor to pull his face off and reveal another actor's underneath.

The Techniques. POV: When Phelps is watching his team, he sees what they see through the cameras embedded in their spectacles. His death only works because Ethan sees it, in turn, purely from Phelps' perspective, and it's amazing what the human eye can miss! When Ethan goes to see Max, his encounter with her lieutenant is entirely seen from his point of view, right up until the point the mask is pulled over his head. It is important to Ethan that this mask be removed and that he get a good look at his opponent. Phelps' devilish plan unravels when he, rather improbably, stands there and lets Ethan put on his camera glasses. Having gone to quite so much trouble to arrange his own death, this seems nothing if not unlikely. Still, the writers needed to get the conspiracy out of the way so they could get on with the chase!

81

Slow/Fast-Mo: The huge explosion of the aquarium is presented in slow motion, which is particularly helpful since this is actually one of those scenes which happen so fast, we need to be able to get a good look to see just what is going on. At the very apex of one of the tensest scenes in De Palma's canon, Krieger drops his knife and we watch it tumble in agonisingly sharp focus and torturous slow motion.

Stories Within Stories: Daringly, the film's title sequence emulates that of the original sixties television series, by featuring images from key moments of the story, including the moment where the bad guy is revealed. These images are edited together so swiftly, you need a pretty good freeze-frame on your video to catch them, but they're there! Immediately after this, Phelps receives his orders via a video which he watches, screen-in-screen.

Split-Screen: Thanks to modern technology, the split-screen image has become commonplace on closed-circuit televisions and on computer monitors. De Palma employs split-dioptre lenses to emphasise the precariousness of Ethan's situation, when he hangs upside down above Donloe's head.Later, when Kittridge is disposing of Donloe, he is way, way, way in the background, almost pushed off the side of the frame. Phelps' explanation of what he says happened, plays out against Ethan's simultaneous realisation of what really happened. Because he was restrained (mostly by his star/producer Cruise, I suspect) to keeping the film as mainstream as possible – this perfect opportunity for use of split-screen was missed.

Long Takes/Tracking Shots: Although it isn't a single take, the raid on the 'black vault' is worth mentioning because it is an 11 minute sequence without a single significant line of dialogue. Thanks to the new computerised editors' ability to blend shots seamlessly together, De Palma approaches the TGV from a high altitude and, as the train roars through the English countryside, we swoop in low, then alongside, then right up to one of the windows to watch the action inside – a shot which would have been all but impossible to do in the days before CGI (Computer Generated Imaging).

References: The scene of Ethan's interrogation by Max reflects *Scarface*'s opening scene, where Tony is grilled by the cops. The mere presence of Vanessa Redgrave is a reference back to the very roots of De Palma's career, when he was so smitten with *Blow-Up*'s tale of surveillance and deduction - *Blow-Up* featured Ms Redgrave.

Artometer: 1/5

Snake Eyes (1998)

The Cast: Nicolas Cage (Rick Santoro), Gary Sinise[1] (Kevin Dunne), John Heard (Gilbert Powell), Carla Gugino (Julia Costello), Stan Shaw (Lincoln Tyler), Luis Guzman[2] (Cyrus)

The Crew: Director: Brian De Palma, Writers: Brian De Palma & David Koepp,[3] Producers: Brian De Palma & Louis A Stroller[5] & others, Composer: Ryuichi Sakamoto, Cinematographer: Stephen H Burum,[7] Editor: Bill Pankow[6]

The Plot: Rick Santoro is about as bent as cops come then, on his day off, a Senator is shot next to him and he decides he doesn't like the fact that some big conspiracy must have taken place without his knowing. So, he sets about solving the case and, in the process, learns some very painful things about just how craven he really is, and just how pure his friends really are.

The Thickening: Bearing many similarities to Hitchcock's 1948 experiment *Rope* (mostly set in one building, the methodical unravelling of a murder plot, the director's unwillingness to give his editor much to do) this film also marks a new phase in De Palma's career – which you could possibly call Post Success. He has always been proving he can make his own films on his own terms, now he has proven he can make a film as big and as dumb and as conformist as the rest of them. What next? Well, strangely, De Palma's mind seems to be returning to the spiritual subtext of his mid-seventies films *Obsession* and *Carrie*.

Although much of it was lost in a last-minute edit, there was originally a Biblical subtext to this film involving a massive God-like storm coming and cleansing all the evils of men and, after all, it *is* a tale of redemption through sacrifice, of the return, after a fashion, of the prodigal son.

The Themes. Voyeurism/Surveillance: Agent Kevin has tracers on all of his agents, so he knows where they are at all times. This plot device is introduced early on, since it becomes key towards the end. Rick goes to check the fight tape and notices, on the overhead shot, that the fight was thrown. Since the hotel is also a casino, its surveillance systems have "quadruple redundancy." In other words, they miss nothing. When the camera pans over the top of the various hotel rooms, the implication is that the hotel monitors can even see in there. Rick follows Julia from an image on a screen, with the assistance of the running commentary from the surveillance booth, to actually confront her in person.

The Motifs. Colours: The MacGuffin Girl, Julia, in her fake Hitchcockian wig, initially wears all-white, which becomes splashed with blood.

This is to throw doubt on to her motives. Is she evil or misguided or just being manipulated? There is a second girl in the fight scene, a fake red-head, who Kevin uses as a decoy to give him an excuse to leave his ring-side post. The boardroom in which Rick and Dunne discuss tactics, is decorated with a fake orange sunset à la *Scarface* and *Carlito's Way*. The Authorised Personnel area, where Kevin first shows his true colours, is lit red and is underground. Another De Palmanian allusion to hell, methinks.

Doubles: When Rick is pursuing Julia we intercut to Kevin's parallel pursuit of her, because we know now that Kevin's motives are pure malice. Neither Rick nor we viewers yet know her significance. Rick is the exact opposite of Eliot Ness. He is the cop who, for the first time, decides not to take the bribe, not to turn a blind eye. He grows a conscience, and is punished mercilessly for it.

The Techniques. POV: The Senator is rushed out on a stretcher, seen from his own perspective, much as Carlito was in *Carlito's Way*. When we get the flashback to the reverse of the earlier scene with Rick bullying Cyrus, we see it initially from Lincoln's perspective then, when he begins to mirror box, we shift sideways to include both Lincoln and his reflection. We continue to see much of the boxing match from his perspective. Julia is terribly short-sighted so, during her escape, to add tension we repeatedly see the world through her eyes, to emphasise how vulnerable she is. After regaining consciousness, we feel Rick's pain, by seeing though his eyes as he staggers back to Julia.

Slow/Fast-Mo: Inspired by the taunt "Too slow!" the fight shifts to slow motion. Similarly, when we are seeing Julia's flashback, Rick's demand "Hold it right there" causes a freeze-frame.

Stories Within Stories: This film begins with a journalist reporting screen-within-screen about the fight in the ring, and the storm brewing around it. Rick arrives on-screen, fulfilling his desire to get on TV, then the camera pans away from the TV to Ricky for real, and a long take begins.

The incident of the shooting is run and rerun, seen from different perspectives, through different media, again and again. Gradually the flashbacks and witness testimonies combine with the various surveillance films to piece together the jigsaw.

As soon as Kevin is caught by the journalists' cameras, and his identity revealed when he sees the light, he simply gives in (rather as Phelps did before him) and very improbably just turns his back and shoots himself. After all that planning, all that effort and all that death, you would think he would at least go down with a fight. I suspect this rather sudden, albeit shocking, conclusion was forced on the film by the removal of its big storm ending.

Split-Screen: Employing one of his 3D screen-splits, The Senator's narrative and assassination take place in the background, while Rick becomes suspicious of the distractions in the foreground. Employing the split-dioptre lens, we have the "here comes the pain" guy in the background, then the whole mass of the crowd and Lincoln in the foreground. The flashbacks to the shooting build up until we find ourselves watching a split-screen of two different perspectives on the crime, as with the bombing in *Phantom Of The Paradise*.

Long Takes/Tracking Shots: This film begins with 13 minutes of (seemingly) uninterrupted narrative, with De Palma marshalling the vast forces of Hollywood technology (including some very cunning digital editing) to present the longest, most elaborate, most... Hitchcockian sustained shot of his career. To me, this sequence actually goes on so long, it becomes distracting. You find yourself watching every person who walks past the camera, to see it they are taking an edit point with them. Every whip-pan seems to be an edit, every camera flash. In interview, De Palma insists that there were only 3 edits, but looking for them does get in the way of following the developing plot. The film ends as it began, with a distinct absence of editing. After Rick's final soliloquy, we move in slowly on the reconstruction work as the credits roll over a total of seven and a half uncut minutes. I just wish I knew whose ring it is buried in the pillar of concrete, into which we are zooming. So I asked Bill Fentum of 'briandepalma.net.' He admitted that this matter was very far from clear, and he only found out by reading the movie's novelisation: It transpires it is the redhead decoy's ring. Over to Bill: "If you look back at some of her scenes in the flashback, the ring is made very prominent in the frame. I guess part of the implication of the final shot is that the new casino is being built literally upon the bodies of people who were used in Heard and Sinise's scheme. Although it also echoes the final shot of *Sisters*, I don't think it carries as strong an impact, because we just don't have the investment in her character that we did with Philip, the victim in *Sisters*."

References: The girl talking to the Senator wears a fake blonde wig. This not only makes her resemble 'Bobbi' in *Dressed To Kill*, but also puts one in mind of the various blonde fatales in Hitchcock movies. The Senator is shot in a particularly Hitchcockian manner – in public, in a crowd, with the protagonist close enough to get embroiled in the ensuing confusion – not unlike the murder in the United Nations building in *North By Northwest* (1959). The key phrase "Here comes the pain!" was previously heard from Carlito in his hiding place in the pool hall toilet. The motif of playing out the same crime, and seeing it from several different perspectives, one by one, is very indicative of Kurosawa's *Rashomon* (1951) and Kubrick's *The Killing* (1956) as well as relating to *Murder À La Mod*. The hurricane is called Jezebel, as was Kleinfeld's boat in *Carlito's Way*. This is an Old Testament name, and the massive storm sequences which originally brought the film to its conclusion were, I suspect, designed to look like God's judgement on Atlantic City for its gambling and corruption, all of which is swept away as by a Biblical flood. De Palma has actually said that he occasionally visits the casinos of Atlantic City, because he is convinced that is how hell would look.

Artometer: 2/5

The Noughties: Hello, Beautiful

Mission To Mars (2000)

The Cast: Gary Sinise[2] (Jim McConnell), Tim Robbins (Woody Blake), Don Cheadle (Luke Graham), Connie Nielsen (Terri Fisher), Jerry O'Connell (Phil Ohlmyer)

The Crew: Director: Brian De Palma, Writers: Jim & John Thomas & Graham Yost & Ted Tally (uncredited) & David S Goyer (uncredited), Producers: Tom Jacobson and a crew of thousands, Composer: Ennio Morricone,[3] Cinematographer: Stephen H Burum,[8] Editor: Paul Hirsch[10]

The Plot: The first manned flight to Mars ends in disaster when all but one of the crew are killed in a massive dust storm. A second mission is despatched to rescue Luke, the sole survivor, even though the second team knows it will take a year to reach Mars. En route, they encounter just about every obstacle imaginable, lose their spaceship, one of their number *and* crash-land on Mars. But it's all in a good cause. During his year in isolation, Luke has just about figured out what is going on on the planet, so they all return to the site of the first team's death, to unmask the million year-old mysteries buried deep in the heart of the desert.

The Thickening: This is a gorgeous movie. The effects are quite stunningly beautiful! It really is a lesson in just what can be achieved these days, with the ever-advancing march of CGI. Unfortunately, as has happened with many credible film-makers in the past, the particular demands of a science fiction narrative, combined with marshalling such immensely complex special effects sequences, leaves the film curiously cold and characterless. The two crews seem to be little more than ciphers, their fate decided by narrative expediency rather than arising naturally out of their interaction.

The Themes. Voyeurism: This being De Palma territory, it is only fitting that the first visitors to Mars are not humans but remote cameras. Our first view of Mars, therefore, is not by the naked eye.

The Motifs: Following on from the spiritual aspects of *Snake Eyes*, De Palma's dalliances with concepts such a redemption and paradise continue to manifest themselves. On board the ship, Phil is suddenly stigmatised by a miniature meteorite passing through the palm of his hand. To not distract the others from their mission, Woody sacrifices himself by glancing back at Mars, then opening his suit and promptly being turned into a pillar of ice. When they arrive on Mars Luke, the only man on the planet, is found living in a hydroponics lab. A curiously verdant place to find in such a desolate spot. One could almost call it a garden of Eden in the desert. Once they cross the desert, they find a message left by their Creator, explaining precisely where 'we' came from.

Colours: As with *Mission:Impossible*, the good guys wear white.

The Techniques. Stories Within Stories: The bulletins from Mars come back to earth after delay, so the space station team only get to communicate through these packets of time-delayed information. Therefore, they have to watch the mission fall apart in horror, knowing that it has already happened. Jim's memories of Earth are reduced to videos he watches, screen-in-screen, on the ship.

Long Takes/Tracking Shots: This film begins with a long shot as the camera wanders around a party, introducing the different characters. I suspect that now De Palma has a reputation for long shots, that he wants to get them out of the way as early as possible, during the titles even, so we can concentrate on the plot thereafter. This is like Hitchcock and his on-screen cameos.

Thanks again to CGI, De Palma can open a scene out in the depths of space and then move in close to a spaceship and simply fly the camera through its window as if it weren't really there (because it isn't, it was added on afterwards).

References: Given his initial role as the mission specialist who stays behind, Sinise is essentially revisiting his role from *Apollo 13* (1995). Yes, this film heaves with visual references to *2001: A Space Odyssey* (1968). In my opinion De Palma did this deliberately because he knew his would be the first big-budget science fiction film of the 21st century, and therefore would be rubbing shoulders with *2001*'s time-scale. I won't be listing the references to *2001* in any great detail, since many of them are a side effect of De Palma simply presenting space-flight in as feasible a manner as Kubrick did 30 years previously. One point which is worth mentioning is that the different sections of the narrative are separated by inter-title cards, just as they are in *2001*. This technique was first employed by De Palma back in *The Wedding Party*, some 4 years before *2001* was released. So I think we can let him have that one! In an early draft of the script, Luke Graham's name was going to be Luc Goddard, a direct tribute to De Palma's first great cinematic inspiration – the French New Wave direct Jean-Luc Godard. The hydroponics garden Luke grows on Mars has its parallel in the film *Robinson Crusoe On Mars* (1964) where Robinson and his pet monkey survive on plants which grow in water. There are also references to a different literary castaway: When Luke is talking to his young son, he alludes to the fact that they are reading *Treasure Island* together: "I want to find out what happens to old Ben Gunn!" Well, Ben Gunn is stranded on a desert island, to protect its buried treasure. He is there, by himself, for so long, that he goes mad. Much as Luke will when he's stranded on Mars. Among the other obvious references to science fiction films are: The space-walk (*2010* (1984)), the message hidden in a sound signal (*Alien* (1979) & *Contact* (1997)), the 'conversation' with the aliens (*The Abyss* (1989, or 1992 for the special edition)), the meteor which destroys all life (*Armageddon* (1998)) and the pilgrim who stays on board the alien spaceship (*Close Encounter Of The Third Kind* (1977, or 1980 for the special edition) and, of course, *Muppets From Space* (1999)).

Artometer: 2/5

Resource Materials

Filmography

The list of De Palma films presently available on video in the UK is, at best, patchy. Ordinarily I would suggest investing in a DVD player, but the list of De Palma discs presently available in that much superior format, is laughable. Plan B would usually be to buy an American Region 1 player and choose from the vast range of films available over there but, to be honest, the choice of De Palma discs presently available is almost as bad as over here. Anyway, the list of VHS videos presently available in the UK is as follows:

The Wedding Party, TR1044, £10.99.
Greetings, 2 ND043, £12.99.
Obsession, V3398, £10.99.
Carrie (Wide-screen), 16149W, £9.99.
The Fury, 1097S, £10.99.
Scarface, 0448503, £5.99.
The Untouchables (Wide-screen), VHR2775, £11.99.
Raising Cain, 0448223, £5.99.
Carlito's Way, 0444303, £5.99.
Mission:Impossible (Wide-screen), VHR4474, £11.99.
Snake Eyes, D610576, £14.99.

Bibliography

General

Bliss, Michael: *Filmmakers No 6: Brian De Palma*, Scarecrow Press, 1983.

Bouzereau, Laurent: *The De Palma Cut*, Dembner Books, 1988.

Bouzereau, Laurent: *Ultra Violent Movies (From Sam Pekinpah To Quentin Tarantino)*, Citadel Press, 1996.

Dworkin, Susan: *Double De Palma*, Newmarket Press, 1984.

Gelmis, Joseph: *The Film Director As Superstar*, Penguin Books, 1970.

MacKinnon, Kenneth: *Misogyny In The Movies: The De Palma Question*, Delaware / Ontario Film Institute, 1990.

Oldham, Gabriella: *First Cut: Conversations With Film Editors*, University of California Press, 1992.

Pye, Michael & Myles, Lynda: *The Movie Brats: How The Film Generation Took Over Hollywood*, Holt, Rinehart and Winston, 1979.

Salamon, Julie: *The Devil's Candy*, Jonathan Cape, 1991.

Get To Know Your Rabbit

Howard, James: *The Complete Films Of Orson Welles*, Citadel.

Sisters

Rubinstein, R: *The Making Of Sisters, Filmmaker's Newsletter*, September 1973.

Wood, Robin: *American Cinema In The 70s: Sisters, Movie*, No 27/28.

Phantom Of The Paradise

Bartholomew, David: *De Palma Of The Paradise, Cinefantastique*, Vol 4, No 2, 1975.

Margulies, E: *Interview, Action*, September/October 1974.

Obsession

Stuart, A: *Phantoms And Fantasies, Films And Filming*, December 1976.

Carrie

Brown, Royal S: *Considering De Palma, American Film*, July-August 1977.

Childs, Mike: *De Palma Interview, Cinefantastique*, Vol 6, No 1, 1977.

Childs, Mike & Jones, Alan: *Sissy Spacek Interview, Cinefantastique*, Vol 6, No 1, 1977.

Matusa, P: *Corruption And Catastrophe In De Palma's Carrie, Film Quarterly*, Fall 1977.

Pirie, David: *American Cinema In The 70s: Carrie, Movie*, No 25.

The Fury

Irvin, Sam L: *Amy Irving Interview, Cinefantastique*, Vol 6 No 4-Vol 7 No 1, 1978.

Irwin, Sam L: *The Fury Journal, Cinefantastique*, Vol 7, No 2, 1978.

Mandell, Paul: *Interview With Brian De Palma, Filmmakers Newsletter*, May 1978.

Swires, S: *Things That Go Bump In The Night, Films In Review,* August/September 1978.

Dressed To Kill

De Palma, Brian: *A Day In The Life, Esquire,* October 1980.

Gerston, Jill: *De Palma 'Tougher' Than Hitchcock,* Article for *Knight-Ridder News Service,* August 1980.

Rosenthal, David: *De Palma, Director Makes A Killing, Dallas Morning News,* 17 August 1980.

Schiff, Stephen: *Review, Boston Phoenix,* 29 July 1980 (reprinted in *Love And Hisses,* Mercury House, 1992).

Schiff, Stephen: *Review, Boston Phoenix,* 26 August 1980 (reprinted in *Love And Hisses,* Mercury House, 1992).

Sragow, Michael: *Review, Los Angeles Herald Examiner,* 25 July 1980 (reprinted in *Flesh And Blood,* Mercury House, 1995).

Vallely, Jean: *Brian De Palma: The New Hitchcock Or Just Another Rip-Off?, Rolling Stone,* 16 October 1980.

Redress Or Undress, People Magazine, 15 September 1980.

Blow Out

McMcurran, Kristin: *Why No Blow-Ups On Blow Out? People Magazine,* 17 August 1981.

Sragow, Michael: *Review Rolling Stone,* 3 September 1981.

Scarface

Brown , Georgia A: *Obsession, American Film,* December 1983.

Hirschberg, Lynn: *Brian De Palma's Death Wish, Esquire,* January 1984.

Jameson, Richard T: *Review, The Weekly* (Seattle), 14 December 1983 (reprinted in

Flesh And Blood, Mercury House, 1995).

McKelvey Cleaver, Thomas: *Scarface, American Cinematographer,* December 1983.

Mills, Michael: *Brian De Palma Interview, Moviegoer,* December 1983.

Rafferty, T: *De Palma's American Dreams, Sight And Sound,* Spring 1984.

Body Double

Denby, David: *Pornography – Love Or Death?*, *Film Comment*, November/December 1984.

De Palma, Brian: *Twenty Questions*, *Playboy*, February 1985.

Pally, Marcia: *Double Trouble*, *Film Comment*, September/October 1984.

Plummer, William: *Despite His Critics ...*, *People Magazine*, 1984.

The Untouchables

De Palma, Brian: *Guilty Pleasures*, *Film Comment*, June 1987.

Kornbluth, Jesse: *The Untouchables Shot-By-Shot*, *Premiere*, July-August 1987.

Pond, Steve: *The Hero's A Hired Gun*, *Premiere*, September 1987.

Casualties Of War

Hinson, Hal: *Review*, *Washington Post*, 18 August 1989 (reprinted in *Love And Hisses*, Mercury House, 1992).

Hugo, Chris: *Three Films Of Brian De Palma*, *Movie*, Winter 1989.

Ingesoll, Earl G: *The Constitution Of Masculinity In Brian De Palma's Film Casualties Of War*, *Journal Of Men's Studies*, August 1995.

Kael, Pauline: *Review*, *New Yorker*, 21 August 1989.

Muse, Eben J: *The Land Of Nam – Romance And Persecution in Brian De Palma's Casualties Of War*, *Literature/Film Quarterly*, Vol 20, No 3, 1992.

Norman, Michael: *Review*, *New York Times*, Sunday, 13 August 1989.

Pond, Steve: *Casualties Of War, Shot-By-Shot*, *Premiere*, September 1989.

Schickel, Richard: *Review*, *Time*, 21 August 1989 (reprinted in *Love And Hisses*, Mercury House, 1992).

Spear, Bruce: *Political Morality And Historical Understanding In Casualties Of War*, *Literature/Film Quarterly*, Vol 20, No 3, 1992.

Telander, Rick: *Michael J Fox In Your Face*, *Premiere*, October 1989.

Bonfire Of The Vanities

Griffin, Nancy: *Sherman's March*, *Premiere*, December 1990.

White, Armond: *Brian De Palma, Political Filmmaker*, *Film Comment*, May-June 1991.

Raising Cain

Plunket, Robert: *Interview With Brian De Palma, Interview,* August 1992.

Keough, Peter: *Out Of The Ashes, Sight and Sound* Vol 2, No 8, 1992.

Carlito's Way

Biskind, Peter: *The Joy Of Sets, Premiere,* December 1993.

Van Gelder, Sadie: *The Gaffe Squad, Premiere,* March 1994.

Mission:Impossible

Arroyo, Jose: *Mission: Sublime, Sight And Sound,* July 1996.

Friend, Tom: *Man With A Mission, Premiere,* June 1996.

Rynning, Roald: *Mission Briefing, Film Review,* August 1996.

Unreich, Rachelle: *Peeping Tom, Empire,* August 1996.

Snake Eyes

Edwards, Stewart: *Review, Film Review,* December 1998.

Malcolm, Derek: *Review, Midweek,* 2 November 1998.

Naughton, John: *Rebel Without Applause, Empire,* December 1998.

Smith, Adam: *Review, Empire,* December 1998.

Strick, Philip: *Review, Sight And Sound,* November 1998.

Thompson, Anne: *The Filmmaker Series: Brian De Palma, Premiere,* September 1998.

Walker, Alexander: *Review, Evening Standard,* 5 November 1998.

Mission To Mars

Curtis, Quentin: *Hollywood Joins The Space Race, The Daily Telegraph,* March 20, 2000.

Fentum, Bill: *Interview With Brian De Palma On Mission To Mars, Directed By Brian De Palma* Website, March 10, 2000.

Magrid, Ron: *Angry Red Planet, American Cinematographer,* March 2000.

Martin, Kevin H: *Mission Accomplished, Cinefex,* No 81, April 2000.

Websites:

Directed By Brian De Palma: www.briandepalma.net - Run by Bill Fentum, this is building up to be an invaluable directory to each and every De Palma movie. Bill's articles combine his expert knowledge with a vast array of research resources, as well as a recent exclusive interview with De Palma himself. This site also hosts the only De Palma discussion forum, which more than makes up for the absence of any alt.fan groups. Essential.

De Palma A La Mod: www.angelfire.com/de/palma/ - A great resource for up-to-the-minute news about De Palma. Works well as a companion piece to 'Directed By' (although the two sites are completely independent of each other). This is also a great resource for links to other magazines and websites of a filmic bent!

Brian De Palma's Split World: members.xoom.com/gpu/depalmae - This site concentrates on duality in De Palma films. It's a fairly brief site, but filled with food for thought.

Senses Of Cinema: www.innersense.com.au/senses/ - A magazine which includes some serious and insightful articles on De Palma, among many other film-makers and subjects.

Le Paradis De Brian De Palma: www.colba.net/~jecr/

Brian De Palma: E I Suoi Film: utenti.tripod.it/de_palma/index1

Two sites which, I am told, are excellent but, until such time as they are translated into English, I'll just have to take other people's word for that. (Work has already begun on translating Le Paradis into English.)

Phantom Of The Opera: members.home.net/the.paradise/index - A beautiful site, dedicated to De Palma's most... unusual film.

The Essential Library

If you've enjoyed this book, check out the following titles in the Pocket Essentials library:

New This Month:
Brian De Palma by John Ashbrook
The Simpons by Peter Mann

Already Published:
Woody Allen by Martin Fitzgerald
The Slayer Files: Buffy the Vampire Slayer by Peter Mann
Jackie Chan by Michelle Le Blanc & Colin Odell
The Brothers Coen by John Ashbrook & Ellen Cheshire
Dr Who by Mark Campbell
Film Noir by Paul Duncan
Terry Gilliam by John Ashbrook
Heroic Bloodshed edited by Martin Fitzgerald
Alfred Hitchcock by Paul Duncan
Stanley Kubrick by Paul Duncan
David Lynch by Michelle Le Blanc & Colin Odell
Noir Fiction by Paul Duncan
Orson Welles by Martin Fitzgerald

Published Next Month:
Vampire Films by Michelle Le Blanc & Colin Odell
Stephen King by Peter Mann

Available at all good bookstores at £2.99 each, or order online at **www.pocketessentials.com**, or send a cheque to:

Pocket Essentials (Dept BP),
18 Coleswood Rd, Harpenden,
Herts, AL5 1EQ, UK

Please make cheques payable to 'Oldcastle Books.' Add 50p postage & packing for each book in the UK and £1 elsewhere.

US customers should contact Trafalgar Square Publishing, tel: 802-457-1911, fax: 802-457-1913, e-mail: tsquare@sover.net